Through the Catechism with Father Champlin

A Question-and-Answer Guide

Joseph M. Champlin

LIGUORI
PUBLICATIONS

One Liguori Drive
Liguori, MO 63057-9999
(314) 464-2500

Imprimi Potest:
James Shea, C.SS.R.
Provincial, St. Louis Province
The Redemptorists

Imprimatur:
Paul A. Zipfel, V.G.
Auxiliary Bishop, Archdiocese of St. Louis

The forty "Companions to the *Catechism*" of section 2 originally appeared
as weekly columns in the *Catholic Sun,* the Syracuse diocesan paper, in
1994–95.

The discussion questions first appeared in a "Video and Discussion Guide"
as a print companion to an hour-long video on the *Catechism.* They
have been augmented by questions developed for the faculty of Bishop
Grimes School in Syracuse by Christine Arabik.

ISBN 0-89243-907-6
Library of Congress Catalog Card Number: 95-82113

Printed in the United States of America
00 99 98 97 96   5 4 3 2 1
First Edition

Cover design by Grady Gunter

CONTENTS

INTRODUCTION

THIS BOOK is primarily for people who have heard or glanced at commentaries about the *Catechism of the Catholic Church*, but have never actually read the text.

However, pastors will likewise discover useful material here for the ongoing instruction of their parishioners in the teachings of the *Catechism*.

In addition, small groups assembled for study of the *Catechism* will also find the questions at the end a stimulus for lively discussions.

Section 1 is a brief overview of the entire *Catechism*. It should situate this text for individual students, parish clergy, and discussion-group participants by sketching the document's origin, language, and overall thrust.

Section 2, the heart of this book, contains forty summaries of the *Catechism* in question-and-answer format, with an assigned reading of fifteen to twenty pages from the *Catechism* after each summary. A person should read the summary and then later study the pertinent portion of the *Catechism*.

Completing one of these summaries and the assigned bite-size reading from the *Catechism* every week will enable the student to finish the entire *Catechism of the Catholic Church* in less than a year.

Section 3 has a series of discussion questions for use after reading the overview and after studying each of the *Catechism*'s four parts.

Michael Jordan learned at an early age that by establishing short-term, doable goals, he could accomplish something of value and draw from that success encouragement to pursue a long-term, more ambitious achievement. Reading through the entire *Catechism of the Catholic Church* is a long-term, ambitious goal. By following through with these brief weekly tasks—short-term, doable goals—within a year you, too, will be proud of a significant achievement in your spiritual life.

SECTION 1
A BRIEF OVERVIEW

We need a catechism for the universal Church which will be biblical, liturgical, sound and practical. It must be rich with scriptural texts, reflect the developments of our liturgy since the Second Vatican Council and respond with clear instruction to the challenges facing contemporary Catholics.

THAT SUGGESTION surfaced at the 1985 Synod of Bishops in Rome. Pope John Paul II accepted the recommendation and in 1986 appointed a commission of twelve cardinals and bishops, chaired by Cardinal Joseph Ratzinger, to undertake the monumental task. The commission in turn assembled an editorial committee of seven diocesan bishops, each with special expertise in theology and catechesis, to assist them with this project.

In today's society, almost no documents of significance appear in final form without passing through the crucible of an extended consultation process. This was certainly true of the *Catechism of the Catholic Church.* It underwent nine successive drafts. Theologians, scriptural scholars, and catechists as well as bishops throughout the entire world examined these versions, contributed comments, and helped make the final text a better one.

On October 11, 1992, the thirtieth anniversary of the opening of the Second Vatican Council, Pope John Paul II published the massive work through an Apostolic Constitution, *Fidei Depositum,* or "Deposit of the Faith."

The authors and the Holy Father did not envision this *Catechism* as a publication designed for popular use. They would not, for example, expect instructors of high school students to use it as a textbook, or even leaders of the Rite for the Christian Initiation of Adults to employ the *Catechism* as the core volume for participants.

Instead, Pope John Paul II views the *Catechism of the Catholic Church* as a "sure and authentic reference text for teaching Catholic doctrine and particularly for preparing local catechisms."

The huge, instant sales of the publication here and abroad indicate, however, that the *Catechism* may be more of a "popular" book than anticipated. Moreover, certain Church leaders think that it will appeal to a wide audience and even urge its extensive distribution.

Cardinal Archbishop William Keeler of Baltimore observed, "In previous centuries relatively few people would have had the theological knowledge or even the basic literacy to make use of this catechism's predecessors. Happily this is no longer the case, so we can commend the catechism to a very large portion of God's people as directly useful to them."

Cardinal Archbishop Roger Mahony of Los Angeles said, "It is my personal goal to have the *Catechism of the Catholic Church* in every Catholic home in the Archdiocese of Los Angeles."

English Translation

The final Latin version of the *Catechism* has yet to be prepared. Translators have been working from an official French version.

In the early stages those working on an English translation attempted to deal with the thorny question of inclusive language. They sought to follow a moderate course in the matter. These scholars expressed references to human persons in a nonexclusive manner, but did not modify references to God whether direct or indirect.

To illustrate: Instead of "Beyond the natural knowledge that every man can have...," the initial version read, "Beyond the natural knowledge that everyone can have...." On the other hand, "God is the sovereign master of his plan" retains the customary "his."

Subsequently, however, the direction shifted, and the approved translation, primarily the work of Hobart, Australia, Bishop Joseph D'Arcy, reverted to the more traditional exclusive language.

Advocates of inclusive language have expressed anger and disappointment over this development. They regret the publication of such an important Church document in an English version that employs exclusive words.

Pope John Paul II responded to the criticism by recalling that this *Catechism* should be an effective and all-encompassing point of reference or source book for local catechisms. These, the Holy Father says, will have their "own catechetical and pastoral language and methods."

In other words, in the United States we likely will soon see adapted catechisms that look to the *Catechism of the Catholic Church* as a resource but apply it to American needs and express its concepts in inclusive language.

Readable Text

Although some people are annoyed that the translation is not inclusive, the more significant observation is that the new *Catechism* is quite readable.

The style is contemporary, with short sentences and clear word usage. If some parts slow the reader down, the problem rests with the content, not the translation.

Often the wording seems quite modern. For example, the angel spoke to "Joseph about Mary his fiancée." That has a current ring to it. I can't recall seeing before a reference to Our Lady as the fiancée of Joseph.

General Observations

The *Catechism* is a weighty volume of 803 pages—with 688 pages of text and 115 pages of references, index, and the like. I offer here three general reflections about the *Catechism,* observations based on my experiences as a pastor of a large 1,850-family parish, a priest for forty years, and a student of the entire text.

1. Following the Church's customary manner, the Catechism *steers a middle course or a centrist position on doctrinal issues and behavioral norms.*

There are countless illustrations in the Church's long history of this *"via media,"* or balanced approach, on matters of doctrine and morality.

In the early Christian centuries, bitter disputes flared over Jesus' nature. Was he truly God? Was he truly a man? Some extremists denied Christ's divinity; others denied his humanity. In time, the Church declared its understanding that he was both God and Man, one Person, but with two natures, divine and human. As we pray in today's liturgy, "Lord Jesus, you are Son of God and Son of Mary."

Similarly, the attitude of Catholics toward the Eucharist as a sacred banquet can affect their behavior at worship. Overemphasize the sacred dimension, and we would experience delayed and infrequent Communion similar to patterns that existed at the start of this century. Overemphasize the banquet dimension, and we may discover careless and casual receptions of the Eucharist without preparation of heart and body.

This centrist approach on doctrinal issues is illustrated by the *Catechism's* discussion of the words we use to describe God. Do we call God "Father," "Mother," both, or neither? The *Catechism* reminds us that human words always fall short of the mystery of God (Article 42; hereafter, only the article number will be given: e.g., #42). It then goes on to describe how the name "Father" conveys certain characteristics of God, and how the image of motherhood communicates others as well (#239). Both militant feminists and extreme traditionalists will very likely find this teaching objectionable. It steers a middle course between them.

This centrist approach on behavioral norms is exemplified by the *Catechism's* instruction on care for the terminally ill. Ordinary care cannot be legitimately interrupted. However, discontinuing medical procedures that are burdensome, dangerous, extraordinary, or disproportionate can be legitimate (#2277–2279). This position again follows a middle path—a balanced view between right-to-die assisted-suicide advocates and those who demand that everything must be done to keep any person alive.

2. The Catechism *will help pastors and their pastoral staff harmonize the quite divergent theologies and spiritualities in a parish.*

Sincere but confused religion teachers in parishes sometimes ask today, "Do we still believe in original sin? Is baptism necessary to get to heaven? Does the Church continue to talk about limbo for deceased unbaptized babies?" Some people have attended courses in which instructors even deny or downplay the notion of original sin.

The *Catechism* clearly upholds the notion of original sin, terming the concept "an essential truth of the faith" (#388). On the other hand, it describes the rich additional effects of baptism beyond the removal of original sin (#1262–1274). Moreover, it never mentions "limbo" but treats in a comforting way the destiny of children without baptism (#1261).

Every parish seems to include people with very differing styles of prayer and spirituality. These contrasting and sometimes conflicting trends can clash over the importance of the reported Marian revelations occurring throughout the United States. The *Catechism* recalls the traditional Church teaching that no new "public" or necessary revelation has been given in our time and that desiring such visions can be foolish and even offensive to Christ. But it acknowledges that "private" revelations have and can be helpful under certain circumstances in living out the gospel (#65–67).

3. Certain elements of the Catechism *will face stiff opposition among some in the United States.*

The *Catechism*'s instruction on sexuality, for example, will and already has drawn criticism from couples who are living together or from persons promoting gay rights.

Similarly, its guidance about the treatment of animals will make Americans uncomfortable or annoyed who have an exaggerated devotion to pets or who object to the use of animals for food or clothing.

Over the next months, as we examine further details of the *Catechism of the Catholic Church,* these three observations will be exemplified again and again in very practical ways. It will become clear how this text does offer sure and authentic, even if controversial, down-to-earth guidance for Catholics seeking to follow Christ in today's complex world.

SECTION 2
A COMPANION
TO THE *CATECHISM*

THIS SECTION contains forty commentaries on the *Catechism* in question-and-answer format. Each commentary covers approximately twenty pages of the *Catechism* and treats the articles cited at the end of the particular commentary. A person should first read the commentary and then the pertinent articles of the *Catechism*. One who follows this process on a weekly basis will, of course, complete the entire *Catechism* in less than a year. Numerical references, as noted earlier in the commentaries, refer to articles in the *Catechism of the Catholic Church*.

APOSTOLIC CONSTITUTION AND PROLOGUE

Commentary 1

Q. How did this new *Catechism* originate?

A. At the 1985 Synod of Bishops in Rome, several participants expressed a desire and need for a universal catechism that would be biblical and liturgical, contain sound doctrine, and respond to the present life of Christians. Pope John Paul II accepted that recommendation and implemented it.

Q. Was there an extensive process in composing the *Catechism?*

A. The Holy Father appointed a commission of twelve cardinals and bishops under Cardinal Ratzinger's direction to undertake the task. The commission in turn engaged seven diocesan bishops with expertise in catechetics and theology to serve as an editorial committee. They, of course, tapped into the talents of specialists for specific ideas and the actual writing. There was considerable consultation, with the document moving through nine drafts before reaching the final form.

Q. Did Pope John Paul II take an active part in the writing or simply approve and sign the text?

A. I can't answer that with any authority, but anyone who has read his other pastoral letters will recognize some of Pope John Paul II's favorite words or phrases in the *Catechism,* like "definitive," "concrete," and "authentic." Such words suggest that he very carefully examined the manuscript in its developing stages.

Q. When was it finally published?

A. On October 11, 1992—the thirtieth anniversary of the opening of the Second Vatican Council—Pope John Paul II published the *Catechism* through an Apostolic Constitution titled "The Deposit of Faith." The current official version is in French; the final edition will be published in Latin later.

Q. Why was there such a delay before the English version appeared?

A. In preparing an English translation, the committee, under the direction of a bright young priest from Savannah, Georgia, encountered objections to certain parts of their work and the use of inclusive language. Thus revisions and a second draft were required before approval and publication, all of which took time. The exclusive language used in the text troubles many people in the United States. Pope John Paul II, however, has mentioned that a later version specifically for this country is both possible and desirable, and such an edition could correct that matter.

Q. What is the *Catechism*'s goal or purpose?

A. The Holy Father hopes that it will "serve as a sure and authentic resource text for teaching Catholic doctrine and preparing local catechisms."

Q. How many parts does the new *Catechism* contain?

A. Four main parts: "The Profession of Faith," "The Celebration of the Christian Mystery," "Life in Christ," and "Christian Prayer."

Recommended Reading

The "Apostolic Constitution" and articles 1–25.

PART ONE: THE PROFESSION OF FAITH
Section One: "I Believe"—"We Believe"

Commentary 2: Our Capacity for God, and God Comes to Meet Us

Q. Does the Catechism speak to me as an individual or to me only as a member of a large group?

A. Both. Section one of the first book, or part, is titled "I Believe—We Believe." "I Believe" reminds us that faith is personal and individualized. The Apostles' Creed expresses that notion. "We Believe" reminds us that our faith comes to us from others and is the faith of a wider group, a community of believers called the Church. The Nicene Creed we recite on Sunday reflects that concept.

Q. Will the Catechism end the controversy on how to address God—as Father, Mother, or otherwise?

A. No. It does, however, repeat a commonly accepted notion that God transcends all creatures and that our human words fall short of the divine mystery. Thus, neither "Father" nor "Mother" nor any other term adequately conveys the notion of who God is.

Q. Can we find any guidance in the Catechism for evaluating the many alleged appearances of Mary in the United States?

A. Yes. The *Catechism* stresses that "public" revelations from God ended with John the Evangelist and the last book of the Bible. God has disclosed nothing essentially new or necessary for our salvation since that time. To be preoccupied or even obsessed with the latest "private" revelation (for example, those in New Jersey, Kentucky, Georgia, or Arizona) could be spiritually unwise.

The mystic and theologian St. John of the Cross even warned that those desiring some vision or revelation would be guilty of foolish behavior and even of offending God. By so doing, he said, they fail to have their eyes fixed totally upon Christ and are living with a desire for some novelty.

Nevertheless, the Church does acknowledge that "private" revelations could help a person or a nation in a particular period of history live out Christ's message. Still, these apparitions should be approached with caution and with a spirit of discernment.

Q. What are the official ways in which God speaks to us today?

A. We can discover God's authentic revelation through the written word of the Bible and the spoken tradition of the Church. Both must be accepted and honored with equal devotion and reverence.

Q. How do we know which books make up the Bible?

A. In the first Christian centuries, the Church determined that point and established a complete list of inspired texts called the canon of Scripture. It includes forty-six Old Testament and twenty-seven New Testament books. Older Protestant Bibles differ slightly from the Catholic Bible, omitting, for various reasons, certain texts like the book of Maccabees and the letter of James.

Q. Are Catholics encouraged to read the Bible?

A. Absolutely. St. Jerome said that ignorance of the Scriptures is ignorance of Christ. St. Thérèse of Lisieux, the Little Flower, remarked, "Above all it's the Gospels that occupy my mind when I'm at prayer....I'm always finding fresh lights there, hidden and enthusiastic messages."

Recommended Reading

Articles 26–141.

Commentary 3: Our Response to God

Q. What do we mean by faith?

A. Part one of the new *Catechism* is titled "The Profession of Faith" and dedicates an extensive section to the nature of faith. Years ago Bishop Frank Harrison of Syracuse, New York, used the following definition, or better, description, of faith. "Faith," he said, "is that which enables us to look beyond and see something more."

Q. Would you clarify that description of faith?

A. We look beyond this object or that experience and discover the presence of God.

For example, three people might be sitting by the side of a lake as a glorious sunset emerges to the west. One person, preoccupied with other matters, never even notices the marvelous sight. A second person gasps, "What a magnificent sunset!" The third person pays attention to the scene, admires the beauty of it, and then exclaims, "Praise God from whom all blessings flow." They all experience the identical reality. One, however, gifted with faith, goes beyond the externals and finds God, the all-powerful and wise maker behind the beauty.

Q. Do you have any other examples of this "looking beyond" to discover God?

A. Many. We can connect with the divine presence, among other ways, in burdens, blessings, and the Church's liturgical celebrations. For example, a Jesuit theology professor teaching at a secular university asked his students what event or situation most often led them to God. The nearly universal response was "suffering." If we recognize suffering not so much as a problem to be solved but as a mystery to be experienced, then our faith will penetrate the maze of difficulties and find a caring God there.

So, too, when people see evidence that prayers have been answered, they frequently find their faith in God has been resurrected or deepened.

Finally, the *Constitution on the Sacred Liturgy* of the Second Vatican Council teaches us that Christ is present in many ways during our liturgical celebrations— in the Eucharist, in the sacraments, in the community gathered for worship, and in the Scriptures. The liturgy is essentially a meeting with Christ in which we connect with the Risen Lord.

Q. Are there models of this type of faith?

A. The *Catechism* cites many Old Testament models of such "looking beyond" faith but asserts that Mary, the mother of Jesus, possessed the purest realization of faith.

Q. Is there a strong Marian component in the *Catechism?*

A. Mary's presence in the *Catechism of the Catholic Church* is what I would call strong and soft. Strong in that the text does have an extended, specific section about Mary; soft in the fact that brief references to the Blessed Virgin are scattered throughout the book.

Q. How does one obtain this gift of faith?

A. Religious faith, the faith we speak of as Catholics, is a pure gift of God. We can, however, dispose ourselves for that gift and strengthen the faith we have by our prayers. The gift is a mysterious blessing from the Lord and requires our free acceptance. For that reason, we should avoid exerting any pressure on people to believe or to enter the Church. Invite them. Accompany them. Support them. But do not try to compel them.

Recommended Reading

Articles 142–84.

Section Two: The Profession of the Christian Faith

Commentary 4: Our Creeds: God Is One and Father

Q. Where does the word *creed* come from?

A. The Latin verb *credo* means "I believe." A creed, therefore, is a formula that summarizes what I or we believe.

Q. What are the main creeds we use in the Church?

A. The Apostles' Creed, "I believe," takes its name from the fact that it was composed during the earliest years of the Church, the Apostolic Era, and reflects the faith of the twelve apostles. The Nicene Creed, "We believe," was developed by the bishops meeting at the Council of Nicaea in 325 as they responded to the particular challenges of those times.

Q. Do these Creeds express everything we believe?

A. They explicitly name the main teachings of our faith and implicitly contain all of the truths we believe as Catholics. For example, neither Creed expressly mentions the Holy Eucharist, which holds such a central place in both our beliefs and worship. But the final phrases beginning, "We believe in the Holy Catholic Church..." imply faith in this truth.

Q. How is the Creed divided?

A. The Apostles' Creed, whose framework and content provides the outline for part one, "The Profession of Faith," of the *Catechism*, contains a dozen articles, a symbolic number connected, obviously, with the twelve apostles.

Q. Is our God an anonymous, powerful force or a personal, caring being?

A. The *Catechism* is blunt about this: God has a name; God is not an anonymous force.

Q. What is that name?

A. God revealed the divine name as YHWH (Yahweh), a Hebrew word that means "I am who am," "I am who I am," "I am he who is," or "I am." Out of respect for the holiness of God's name, however, the people of Israel do not pronounce this name. Instead they replace it by the divine title "Lord." We see that in our prayer, *"Kyrie, eleison,"* or "Lord, have mercy."

Q. Why do some people call God "Father" or "Mother"?

A. Many religions address God as "Father." Jesus, however, revealed God as his father and our father in a unique and personal way. Speaking of God as "Father" conveys the notion that God is the origin of everything and an authority beyond us. At the same time, the title communicates God's goodness and loving care for us.

On the other hand, the image of God as a mother emphasizes the Lord's dwelling within us and the Lord's tenderness. There are many biblical references to the maternal dimensions of God.

Q. Could that be a problem for people who have suffered under abusive fathers or mothers?

A. Yes. But we need to realize that God is neither man nor woman. God has no gender. God transcends, or far surpasses, human fatherhood or motherhood. For people so troubled, they may wish to concentrate upon Jesus, who said, "The Father and I are one" and "Whoever sees me sees the Father."

Q. Do you have suggestions for a prayer honoring the Trinity?

A. Two of them. Most commonly, the sign of the Cross ("In the name...") symbolizes one God and three Persons as we trace the gestures upon ourselves. The other would be "Glory Be to the Father, the Son, and the Holy Spirit, as it was, is now, and will be forever."

Recommended Reading

Articles 185–267.

Commentary 5: God, the Almighty and Creator

Q. What are some of the words we use to describe God?

A. Two encompassing attributes of God are "almighty" and "creator." We believe that our God can do all things and has made the world (and everything within it) from nothing.

Q. How do we know where the world came from and where it is going?

A. Our human reason has the ability to discover the existence of God as well as the creation of the world and its destiny. However, because of our flawed nature, individual knowledge can be erroneous or obscure. Scripture, especially the first three chapters of Genesis, helps us here. Our vision of the beginning and end of this world becomes clearer as we study the biblical message.

Q. Are we obligated to follow any particular theory of the world's development?

A. No. The Bible is a religious book, not a scientific treatise. As long as we hold fast to the fundamental truths of the scriptural accounts, we are free to accept any of the various theories advanced to explain how the created world arrived at its developed state.

Q. Is the spiritual world good and the material world bad?

A. Not according to Catholic beliefs. In its history the Church has always struggled with those who taught, on the one hand, that only the material world is real, and with those who, on the other hand, taught that only the spiritual world is important. The new *Catechism* reminds us that all of creation is good and is a mysterious mix of the spiritual and material.

Q. Do you have any comment about those who argue that God is the earth or our planet or the world around us?

A. That would be a risky and nebulous approach to God. The Church teaches that God transcends all creation but is present to it. God is in the world but beyond it. Without this distinction we slip into a variety of false and ultimately destructive ways of thinking and acting.

Q. If God is good, powerful, and loving, how do we explain so much suffering and such great pain or evil in the world?

A. Catholic doctrine teaches that, wonder of wonders, God has given us freedom of choice. We can thus choose to be good or bad, to love or hate, to follow divine rules or reject them, to make correct or incorrect decisions. Many, probably most, of the troubles in this world can be traced to poor human choices. God could have produced a perfect, flawless universe; instead, God, respecting our freedom, allows us to mess up the beautiful world made for us.

Q. What does the Bible mean when it says, "For those who love God all things work together for good"?

A. God does not will or want sin and suffering. But when these occur, God continues to be present, even especially close to the broken-hearted, bringing good out of the bad. Some prayerful reflection often reveals how that has happened in particular situations.

Recommended Reading

Articles 268-324.

Commentary 6: Angels, Our Creation, and Our Fall

Q. Did devotion to the angels decline after the Second Vatican Council?

A. That would seem to be the case. Many older Catholics who believe in angels and remember the Guardian Angel Prayer admit that today they seldom, if ever, call upon angels for help.

Q. What is that prayer?

A. This is the traditional Guardian Angel Prayer—"Angel of God, my guardian dear, to whom God's love commits me here, ever this day be at my side, to light and guard, to rule and guide."

Q. Isn't there a current resurgence of interest in angels?

A. Definitely. Surveys show a large majority of Americans now believe in angels, an increase over recent years. Books about angels have been on secular bestseller lists for months. Religious gift stores and novelty shops contain all types of angelic artifacts. Magazines like *Time* feature cover stories about these spiritual beings.

Q. Don't we have many references to angels in the Bible and the liturgy?

A. Yes. Almost every page of sacred Scripture—both Old and New Testaments— contains mention of an angel or angels. Our liturgy has feasts celebrating guardian angels (October 2) and archangels (September 29), a votive Mass honoring the angels, and frequent inclusion of angels in the prayers of the Eucharist.

Q. How does the new *Catechism* treat angels?

A. In eight paragraphs and three pages, it states that the existence of angels is a truth of faith. Moreover, it describes these purely spiritual creatures as personal and immortal beings with intelligence and will who surpass in perfection all visible creatures. Finally, it teaches that each one of us has an angel as a protector and shepherd leading us to life. Thus from infancy to death we are surrounded by the watchful care and intercession of angels.

Q. What is the relationship of human beings to the rest of creation?

A. The *Catechism* establishes a simple but far-reaching principle: God created everything for human beings; it is our vocation to subdue the earth as God's stewards, but in a reasoned and constructive, not an arbitrary and destructive, way. Animal-rights activists very likely would disagree on that point.

Q. Is God a man or a woman, male or female?

A. Neither. God is pure spirit in which there is no place for differences between the sexes. However, the "perfections" of a husband and father, wife and mother do reflect in a partial way God's perfections.

Q. Are there insights in the *Catechism* for parents?

A. Yes. The Church teaches that God immediately and directly creates the soul, the spiritual principle of every human being. Conception therefore involves three persons—the father, the mother, and God.

Q. Do we still believe in the devil, or Satan?

A. The Church teaches that Satan was at first a good angel, made by God, who rebelled and rejected the Creator and in powerful but limited ways works against God's plan for us. Satan can influence and affect us but not take away our freedom. Why God allows such diabolical activity and how this plays out in the world are mysteries that will only be understood later in the life to come.

Recommended Reading

Articles 325–421.

Commentary 7: Jesus Christ—Truly Divine and Truly Human

Q. What is the meaning of the name *Jesus?*

A. In Hebrew, the name or word means "God saves." The angel told Joseph, "You are to name him Jesus, because he will save his people from their sins" (Matthew 1:21). That is his identity, Savior, and his mission, to save us.

Q. Don't we use the name often in prayer?

A. Certainly. Our worship prayers frequently conclude, "Through our Lord Jesus

Christ." The Hail Mary mentions "the fruit of thy womb, Jesus." It occurs in the oriental prayer of the heart, "Lord, Jesus Christ, Son of God, have mercy on me, a sinner." Blessed Kateri, the Native American saint, carved "Jesus" on a tree along the Mohawk to help her pray.

Q. Does oil have special significance in the Bible?

A. Yes. Many religions, including the Jewish tradition as well as our Roman Catholic practice, feature anointing with oil as part of their rituals. Priests, prophets, and kings were anointed in the Old Testament. Jesus in the New Testament is the priest, prophet, and king "par excellence." He is understandably thus called Christ, which means "the anointed one." As his followers, we Christians likewise are the anointed ones since we share in Jesus' life and roles through baptism and are anointed with the chrism oil during that ceremony.

Q. Why do we speak of God and Jesus as "Lord"?

A. God revealed to Moses that the divine name in Hebrew is YHWH (Yahweh). The Jewish people out of respect never pronounced that word. Instead, they would speak of God as Lord, or, in Greek, "Kyrios." "Lord," now applied to Jesus, refers to his divinity. We, of course, employ that phrase repeatedly in prayer. *"Kyrie, eleison,"* or "Lord, have mercy," occurs during the Eucharist. "Through Christ our Lord" often surfaces as a conclusion to prayers. "My Lord and my God" is a favorite personal aspiration of people at the consecration of Mass. The presiding priest at worship greets us regularly with "The Lord be with you."

Q. Is Jesus God or man?

A. After many debates in the early Christian centuries the Church clarified this discussion by finally declaring that Christ is truly God and truly man, truly divine and truly human. One of the greetings at the penitential part of Mass mirrors this teaching: "Lord Jesus, you are Son of God and Son of Mary."

Q. Did Jesus know the future?

A. That is a complex question with no easy answers. As Son of God with a divine nature, Christ knows everything. But as Son of Mary the Bible tells us he grew in "age, wisdom, and grace." How do you harmonize those two qualities? In Gethsemane, for example, did Jesus know exactly what was going to happen on the cross? On the cross, was Christ fully aware that he would rise three days later? Theologians speculate on these questions, but no certain response should be expected. We are in the area of mystery.

Recommended Reading

Articles 422–83.

Commentary 8: Son of Mary

Q. Does the *Catechism* discuss Mary, the mother of Jesus, at length?

A. Earlier, we saw that the *Catechism* contains a soft Marian element: that is, there are brief references to Our Lady throughout the text. However, it also possesses a strong Marian dimension, with twenty paragraphs (#487–507) examining in some detail what the Church believes about Jesus' mother.

Q. Are there instances of a feminine element in this document?

A. Yes. For example, the *Catechism* mentions the mission of numerous holy women who prepared the way for Mary's role. It cites, in this context, Eve, Sarah, Hannah, Deborah, Ruth, Judith, Esther, and "many other women."

Q. What do we mean by the development of doctrine?

A. There are many truths of our faith that have always been implicitly believed and honored in the Church's worship and teaching, but whose clearer and explicit expression evolved centuries after the time of Christ. To illustrate that point, the Church from its beginning acknowledged that Mary was "full of grace." However, it gradually came to understand how this signified, among other things, that she was saved from sin or redeemed from the first moment of her conception. That led eventually to Pope Pius IX's formal definition in 1854 of Mary's Immaculate Conception.

This was not a new revelation from God, only the more precise understanding and more explicit expression of a truth always present in the Church's tradition.

Q. How is Joseph described?

A. As Jesus' legal father. Mary is also named as "his fiancée."

Q. When did belief in Mary's virginity start?

A. From the Church's earliest years. For instance, St. Ignatius of Antioch, at the beginning of the second century, expressed his faith that Jesus was "truly born of a virgin." Soon the Church summarized its teaching about Mary's virginity by declaring Our Lady was a virgin before, during, and after the birth of Christ.

Q. Isn't this in contradiction to the New Testament passages that mention Jesus' brothers and sisters?

A. No. The original biblical words for brothers or sisters can mean true blood brothers or sisters, but they also can denote close relatives according to an Old Testament expression. Moreover, two brothers mentioned, James and Joseph, are even described in the Bible as sons of another or "the other" Mary. The Church thus interprets these and other similarly identified persons as close relatives of Christ, but Jesus as Mary's only child.

Q. Why are churches today building baptismal fonts that are almost swimming pools?

A. The Church prefers baptismal immersion, or the plunging of infant or adult into water for the sacrament. Nevertheless, it permits infusion, or the pouring of blessed water over the head of the one being baptized. Immersion symbolizes more fully our own dying with Christ and rising to new life with him.

In the early era of Christianity immersion was a common practice. It dramatized that our darkness and sin are buried in the waters of baptism and that we rise from those waters to the new life and light of the Risen Jesus.

Recommended Reading

Articles 484–542.

Commentary 9: Jesus Our Savior

Q. What is the Kingdom of God?

A. Jesus' initial public message was "Repent, and believe in the gospel; the kingdom of God is at hand." Christ thus came to establish the kingdom of heaven on earth, a foretaste of the kingdom still to come. God wishes us to share in the divine life and does that by gathering people around the Son, Jesus Christ. This gathering we call the Church, which on earth is the seed and beginning of that kingdom of heaven. The kingdom, therefore, is already here, but not yet complete.

Q. Why do we hear about the "paschal mystery" so often?

A. One of the main meanings of the word *paschal* is "passover." It reminds us of the deliverance of the Old Testament Jewish people from pagan bondage in Egypt by the blood of a lamb. An angel of destruction "passed over" those homes whose door posts were sprinkled with the blood of this slain Passover, or paschal, lamb. Jesus is the new lamb of God who has saved us by pouring out his blood on the cross. We often speak of Christ as the paschal, or Passover, lamb. The paschal mystery, therefore, is the mystery of Jesus' coming into this world, dying for us, and rising from the dead, and of his future coming back into the world.

When the priest invites us at Mass to "proclaim the mystery of faith," he is referring to the paschal mystery. Our frequent response "Christ has died, Christ is risen, Christ will come again" succinctly summarizes the meaning of this mystery.

Q. Is twelve a special biblical number?

A. Yes. It occurs often in the Bible. Consider, for example, the twelve tribes of Israel, the twelve apostles, the twelve articles of the Apostles' Creed, and the number of people in heaven described by the Book of Revelation as 144,000, a multiple of 12 and 1,000, also a special figure signifying perfection.

Q. Who is the leader of the apostles?

A. Peter. Every list of the twelve begins with Peter. Peter often is the spokesman for the other apostles. He along with James and John were the favored followers who were with Christ during his transfiguration on Mount Tabor and his agony in Gethsemane. Christ changed his name from Simon to Peter, which means "rock," made him the rock foundation of the Church, established him as the chief shepherd who was to feed the Lord's sheep, and entrusted to him the keys of the kingdom of heaven.

Q. What do you mean by "the keys of the kingdom"?

A. Jesus bestowed upon Peter the promise of the keys, symbolizing the power to open and close the gates of God's kingdom and the power to "bind and loose" on earth and in heaven. These notions signify the authority to forgive sins, to pronounce judgments on matters of doctrine, and to make decisions affecting the operation of the Church on earth.

Q. Do we hold the Jews responsible for Jesus' death?

A. No. The *Catechism* recalls that Jesus, and Peter later, accepted the ignorance of the Jews in Jerusalem and even of their leaders. Therefore, they did not lay responsibility for Christ's death upon the Jews of the time. Neither do we place blame upon other Jews of different centuries and places. The *Catechism* also cites the teaching of the Second Vatican Council: "Neither all Jews indiscriminately at that time, nor Jews today can be charged with the crimes committed during his Passion."

Q. Did we contribute to Christ's death on Calvary?

A. Yes. The *Catechism* reminds us that sinners were the authors and ministers of Jesus' sufferings. He endured pain and death for us. Consequently, because of our sins, we bear a serious responsibility for the torments inflicted upon Christ.

Recommended Reading

Articles 543–605.

Commentary 10: The Dying and Rising of Christ

Q. When and how did Jesus establish the Mass and the priesthood?

A. While Jesus was put to death by leaders and soldiers of his time, he in fact freely accepted his passion and crucifixion. The supreme expression of that free offering came at the Last Supper. There, while still free, he transformed this final meal with the apostles into the memorial of his voluntary offering to the Father for our salvation.

He did so with the familiar words "This is my body which is given for you....This is my blood…poured out for many for the forgiveness of sins."

Christ then told the apostles they were to do this in memory of him, to perpetuate this memorial of his sacrifice. He thereby initiated, established, or instituted his apostles as priests of the New Covenant.

Q. Why do we place such stress on crosses and crucifixes?

A. We reverence them because Jesus' passion on the wood of the cross saved us, opened up the doors of heaven for all. A crucifix—that is, a cross with the figure of Christ on it—recalls in a unique way that Good Friday event. Prayers in our worship bring out this truth: "Hail, O cross, our only hope." "We adore you, O Christ, and we praise you, because by your holy cross you have saved the world."

Q. Is it still appropriate to "offer up" our troubles to God?

A. Definitely. In a way unknown to us, but known to God, Jesus associates us with his sufferings on the cross. Consequently, when we unite our own burdens with those of the Savior on the cross, we in some manner are sharing in his work of saving others. Our offered smaller "crosses" became one with the larger cross of Christ.

Mary is the perfect model for us in this regard since she was associated more intimately with the mystery of her son's saving suffering than anyone else has been or will be.

Q. What does the Creed mean by "He descended into hell"?

A. Jesus tasted death in the sense that he experienced the separation of his soul from his body between the time he died on the cross and the time he was raised from the dead. During that interval he visited "hell"—*Sheol* in Hebrew or *Hades* in Greek—the abode of the dead. Christ made that journey not to deliver the damned or to destroy the hell of damnation, but to free the just who had gone before him and were awaiting the Savior's coming.

Q. Did Jesus actually rise from the dead or was that merely a hopeful belief of the early Christians?

A. The *Catechism* summarizes our Church's teaching in this fashion: "The Resurrection was an historical event that could be verified by the sign of the empty tomb and by the reality of the apostles' encounters with Christ." However, it goes on to state that the Resurrection "remains at the very heart of the mystery of faith as something that transcends and surpasses history."

Recommended Reading

Articles 606–67.

Commentary 11: Christ's Second Coming, and The Holy Spirit

Q. What is the real nature of Advent?

A. The Church prepares for three "Advents" or "comings" of Christ during these days: In *history,* as we recall the birth of Jesus in Bethlehem. In *glory,* as we ponder the second coming of the Lord at the end of time to judge the living and the dead. In *mystery,* as we experience the special presence of the Savior in the Eucharist and through the grace-filled liturgies of the Christmas season.

Q. Is there a special prayer for this season?

A. Yes. "Maranatha!" or "Our Lord, come!"

Q. Do we know the day and the hour of Christ's coming?

A. We know neither the exact time of Jesus' coming to take us home individually through our own deaths nor the precise moment of the Lord's coming at the end of the world. Christ said during his life on earth that even he did not know the day or the hour of the end. Furthermore, he cautioned his listeners (and us), "It is not for you to know the times or seasons."

Q. How then should we prepare?

A. Speculation about this or that supposed sign alluded to in the Scriptures or mentioned in private revelations is really useless and a waste of spiritual energy. It would be better to live the present moment fully conscious of God's presence. The lectionary of biblical readings for Mass has these scriptural texts to help us: "Be watchful and ready; pray constantly; be faithful until death; you know not when the Son of man is coming; be worthy to stand before him."

Q. Is the Third Person of the Trinity the Holy Ghost or the Holy Spirit?

A. I am in my sixties, and people of my age were taught during our early years to use the phrase "Holy Ghost." Today "ghost" probably relates more to horror movies and Halloween costumes than to religious realities. Thus, current Catholics almost universally speak of the "Holy Spirit."

Q. Would you explain the phrase "Holy Spirit"?

A. "Spirit" translates the Hebrew word *ruah,* which primarily means breath, air, or wind. Jesus used those metaphors occasionally in teaching about the Spirit. *Holy* and *spirit* are also both considered divine attributes. Therefore, the terms *holy* and *spirit,* linked together and capitalized, indicate the unique third Person of the Trinity.

Q. Are there parallels between the wind and the Spirit?

A. Yes. We cannot actually see the wind, but we can see and hear its power and effects. Consider swiftly moving sailboats, rustling leaves, or rafters creaking in a storm. So, too, with the Holy Spirit.

Q. What are some occasions in which we can experience the Holy Spirit's impact?

A. The Scriptures, the tradition of our Church and the Church's official teachings, our sacramental liturgies, prayer, special talents or gifts and ministries within the Church, signs and wonders, the lives of the saints.

Q. How does the Church communicate to us this invisible Spirit?

A. The Church uses many symbols to represent the Holy Spirit. For example, water, anointing with oil, fire, cloud, light, seal, hand, fingers, and a dove.

Recommended Reading

Articles 668–730.

Commentary 12: The Church

Q. What do the phrases "last days" or "end times" mean?

A. Those words refer biblically and theologically to the time of the Church, that is, the kingdom that Jesus established here on earth, but that will be made perfect only at the end of time. The phrase, however, also sometimes denotes that period around the Second Coming of Christ when this world as we know it will cease.

Q. Is there a connection between Christ and the Church?

A. Yes, an essential one. The Church sees itself as Jesus living in the world today. It has no other light than the light of Christ. Ancient Christian teachers and writers thus compared the Church to the moon whose total light is but a reflection of the sun's rays.

Q. How did the word *church* develop?

A. It comes from Greek and Latin words meaning a convocation or assembly of people, usually for a religious purpose. The Old Testament used the term to describe God's Chosen People, the Israelites. When early Christians applied the word to themselves, they were recognizing or accepting their Jewish heritage. The English word *church* and the German *kirche* derive from another Greek term that means "what belongs to the Lord."

Q. Are there different Catholic Christian understandings of the term *church?*

A. We interpret the word in three ways: to designate the assembly of people gathered for public worship or the liturgy; to denote the local faith community; to describe the community of believers throughout the world.

Q. Can we see the Church or is it totally spiritual and therefore invisible?

A. The Church is both visible and invisible—a complex, mysterious entity. We can see its members, observe its actions, and read its rules. But with the eyes of faith we go beyond those external, visible elements and connect with the spiritual, invisible realities beneath them. To illustrate: we can see, hear, and feel the waters of baptism, but we can also discover underneath through our belief the grace of Christ communicated in that sacrament.

Q. How does the *Catechism* describe the Church?

A. It uses three central images to describe the Church: the People of God, the Body of Christ, and the Temple of the Spirit.

Q. Where did the "People of God" concept originate?

A. In the Old Testament there are occasional references to it. "You will be my people, and I will be your God" is a familiar phrase from the prophet Jeremiah. The Second Vatican Council employed that notion in enriched fashion as its primary image to describe the Church.

Q. What is the significance of the image "Body of Christ"?

A. During the 1940s Pope Pius XII issued an encyclical describing the Church as the Mystical Body of Christ. The document looked to Jesus' words about the vine and the branches and Paul's reference to the Body of Christ—with Jesus as head and we as members—for its basis. This image emphasizes the inner, real bond between ourselves and Christ, and with one another.

Q. Why do we have the new notion of the Church as the Temple of the Holy Spirit?

A. It is not really new, but the contemporary emphasis on the action of the Holy Spirit in our lives makes this image appropriate for today. The Holy Spirit is considered the principle of every vital and saving action of the Church. The Spirit is also behind those many graces and gifts we see operating remarkably within people of the Church during this modern era.

Recommended Reading

Articles 731–96.

Commentary 13: The Church—One and Holy

Q. Would you explain the phrase that we repeat often in the Creed, "The One, Holy, Catholic and Apostolic Church"?

A. Not in a few sentences. The new *Catechism* contains a relatively lengthy section, articles 811–70, to treat this particular phrase. Readers will probably find that portion one of the more interesting and practical parts of part one, "The Profession of Faith."

Q. What do we mean that the Church is "one"?

A. The oneness or unity of the Church has many dimensions. It has one founder (Christ) and one "soul" (the Holy Spirit). It also manifests that oneness or unity through the one faith it has received from the apostles; through its one common celebration of worship, especially the sacraments; and through its apostolic succession, or its origin from the apostles through the sacrament of holy orders.

Q. Why are there so many divisions and such diversity in the Church?

A. The diversity is a great divine blessing. It shows that God has endowed this Church of unity with many different yet rich gifts, talents, offices, conditions, and ways of life. For example, at a recent concelebrated Mass at the Vatican II Institute for clergy in California, I heard the general intercessions spoken by priest participants in five languages.

The divisions are a regrettable human failing. Over the centuries, serious dissensions arose in the Church, and large communities separated from full communion with the Catholic Church. How did this happen? The *Catechism* admits that often people "of both sides were to blame."

Q. Doesn't Christ want unity in his Church?

A. Yes. The *Catechism* proposes several practical ways of achieving this oneness that Jesus desires: a renewal of the Catholic Church and a conversion of heart among its members; common prayer and joint collaboration in works of charity between peoples of different churches; increased understanding of one another, dialogue among theologians, and the ecumenical formation of Catholics, especially priests.

Q. How can we call the Church "holy" when sin mars its past and present?

A. The Church's goal is the holiness of all its members; the Church's teachings and rituals make holiness possible for its members; and in every age there have been holy members or "saints" within the Church.

Yet the Church is human, messy, a mix of saints and sinners.

I think this quote from the *Catechism* is a magnificent and quite realistic description of the holy and not so holy nature of our Church.

The Church, however, clasping sinners to her bosom, at once holy and always in need of purification, follows constantly the path of penance and renewal. All members of the Church, including her ministers, must acknowledge that they are sinners. In everyone, the weeds of sin will still be mixed with the good wheat of the Gospel until the end of time (#827).

Q. Who are these "saints"?

A. They are members of the Church who believed deeply, worked hard at holiness, and never gave up despite their faults, weaknesses, and sins. The Church canonizes some of these people, stating that they are now in heaven and offering them as models and intercessors for us on earth. Jesus' Mother Mary is the epitome of all such saints.

Recommended Reading

Articles 797–856.

Commentary 14: The Church—Catholic and Apostolic

Q. What is the meaning of the word "Catholic Church" found in both the Apostles' and Nicene Creeds?

A. When people use the term "Catholic," they generally are referring to the Roman Catholic Church. For example, "I am a Catholic"; "she goes to Mass at the Catholic church"; "he sends his children to a Catholic school." But in the Creeds, the meaning is wider, signifying "universal."

Q. How is our Church "universal"?

A. We speak of the Church as universal in two ways. First, it contains the fullness of what Christ has given to us for our salvation. Thus, the Catholic Church communicates Jesus' teaching in its entirety and celebrates all of the rites Christ has provided for our spiritual welfare. It has been doing this since its inception at Pentecost and will continue to do so until the Lord's Second Coming at the end of the world.

Q. Has the Catholic Church reached people everywhere?

A. No. But that is its mission and the other meaning of "universal." The Church desires to preach the Good News of Christ to the entire human race and welcomes all peoples into its membership.

Q. Do people who are not "Roman Catholic" belong to the Church?

A. To be a full member of the Catholic Church requires faith, baptism, acceptance of Church rules, and union with the pope. Others, however, belong in varying degrees to the Church depending upon their beliefs and practices.

Q. Could you give examples of this not full but partial belonging to the Church?

A. Those who believe in Christ and are properly baptized (members of most Protestant churches) have a certain, although imperfect, communion with the Church. That is especially close in the case of Orthodox Church members. Those who are not Christians (for example, Jews and Muslims) also are linked in a particular way to the Church because of their beliefs in God, the Old Testament, and other truths we hold in common. Even those whose tenets seem far removed from the teachings of the Catholic Church, but who nevertheless do share similar religious concerns (for example, human origin and destiny, the search for God), also belong in some way to the Church.

Q. Must you, therefore, be a "Catholic" to reach heaven?

A. Not an actual, explicit member. However, our salvation does come from Christ through the Church. But as we have mentioned, human beings can connect with the Savior through the Church in various ways.

Q. What are the requirements for those "outside the Church" to be saved and enter heaven?

A. The *Catechism,* echoing a statement of the Second Vatican Council, puts it this way:

> *Those who, through no fault of their own, do not know the Gospel of Christ or his Church, but who nevertheless seek God with a sincere heart, and, moved by grace, try in their actions to do his will as they know it through the dictates of their conscience—those too may achieve eternal salvation* (#847).

Q. How is the Church "apostolic"?

A. We call the Church apostolic because it has been founded upon the apostles, teaches what they taught, and is guided by them today through the Holy Father and the bishops, their successors.

Recommended Reading

Articles 857–945.

Commentary 15: Communion of Saints, Including Mary;
Forgiveness of Sins; Resurrection of the Body

Q. What do we mean by the "communion of saints"?

A. This phrase has two closely related meanings: communion, or union, with others in holy things and among holy persons.

Q. How are we united with others "in holy things"?

A. We share the gift of faith handed down to us from the apostles; the sacraments; the various graces or talents members possess for building up the Church; our mutual possessions so that no Christian should ever be in need; the spirit of love that binds us together as a living religious body in which the strengths or weaknesses of one member strengthen or weaken all the others.

Q. How are we united with others "among holy persons"?

A. There is a real and alive link or connection between members of the Church on earth, those in what we term purgatory, and the saints in heaven. The *Catechism* describes it this way: Some of Christ's "disciples are pilgrims on earth. Others have died and are being purified, while still others are in glory, 'contemplating God'" (#954).

Q. Can the saints in heaven help us?

A. Yes. When saints lived on earth, they were not perfect persons. However, these people never gave up, always started over, and strove mightily to walk in Christ's footsteps. Thus the saints help human beings here by serving as models for them. Moreover, now that they are with God in heaven, the saints also powerfully pray or intercede for us.

St. Dominic, for example, on his deathbed encouraged members of his religious community with these words: "Do not weep, for I shall be more useful to you after my death and I shall help you then more effectively than during my life."

Q. Is there ever a "second" baptism?

A. Yes and no. The sacrament of baptism, never repeated, cleanses us of all sin. Still, it does not deliver us from the weakness of human nature. Consequently, we continue to make bad choices, stumble, slip, and sin. The sacrament of penance, or reconciliation, forgives those misdeeds. We thus sometimes term that sacrament a second, or laborious, kind of baptism.

Q. Are there any sins that can never be forgiven?

A. None, if one truly repents. Even sins against the Holy Spirit, mentioned in the Scriptures as beyond forgiveness, can be forgiven with proper repentance.

Q. What happens at death?

A. The soul and body separate, with the human body immediately beginning to decay and the human soul instantly going forth to meet God. In some mysterious way, "at the last day" or "the end of the world," the body will rise in glorified fashion and reunite with the soul. For this reason, the Church does not believe in reincarnation after death.

Q. Will I be terrified when my time comes to die?

A. Facing unknown and uncharted waters understandably causes some dying people anxiety and fear. For others, belief in the resurrection eases those negative feelings and makes them joyfully expectant. Two saints, with the same names but with a different spelling—Teresa of Avila and Thérèse of Lisieux—illustrate that point. One remarked, "I want to see God, and in order to see him, I must die." The other commented, "I am not dying; I am entering life."

Recommended Reading

Articles 946–1019.

Commentary 16: Death, Heaven, Purgatory, and Hell

Q. What happens at death?

A. Death is the separation of our soul, the principle of life, from our body. The material body immediately begins to decay, but the spiritual soul at the very moment of death goes before God for what our Church terms the particular judgment.

Q. How are we judged?

A. The great mystic St. John of the Cross once said, "At the ending of life, we shall be judged on our love." According to our good works and faith or according to our bad deeds and disbelief, God compares or refers our lives to Christ. As a consequence of this particular judgment, we then either enter into the blessedness of heaven, through a purification or immediately, or enter everlasting damnation.

Q. Will we reconnect in heaven with our beloved who have died before us?

A. Yes. We call "heaven" the communion of life and love with the Trinity, the Virgin Mary, the angels, and all the blessed. It is the ultimate end and fulfillment of our deepest human longings. There are no more tears, pain, or sorrow. We see the face of God and become partners with all those who believed in him and remained faithful to his will until the end.

In the last weeks of his difficult death through cancer, Father Ron Buckel, a parish priest of our diocese, told visitors that he was excited by the prospects before him. "I have prepared many people for death and am looking forward to reunion with them."

Q. Does the Church still believe in purgatory?

A. Yes again. Those who die in God's grace and friendship, though still imperfectly purified, will eventually attain heaven, but must undergo the purification necessary to achieve the holiness required for the joy of heaven. The Church calls this final purification by the name of purgatory, from the Latin word meaning to purge, cleanse, or purify.

Q. Isn't that a relatively new notion?

A. Yes and no. From its beginning the Church has prayed for those who have died that, should they be in need of purification, their journeys to the vision of God would be hastened by our prayers. We see evidence of this practice in carvings on the walls of the catacombs and a reference to such a procedure in the Old Testament book of Maccabees.

However, the more explicit formulation of the notion took place in later councils of the Church, specifically, those at Florence in 1439 and Trent in 1563.

Q. Is belief in hell part of Catholic teaching?

A. The Church teaches that hell exists and is eternal, and that its chief punishment is separation from God forever, God who alone can satisfy the human heart. Nevertheless, we have no knowledge of who is in hell, and the Church maintains that God predestines no one to this fate. Human beings make that choice on their own.

Q. Where are we now in our study?

A. Nearly halfway done. We have just completed part one, "The Profession of Faith," which is the longest of the four parts. Next we begin part two, "The Celebration of the Christian Mystery."

Recommended Reading

Articles 1020–65.

PART TWO: THE CELEBRATION OF THE CHRISTIAN MYSTERY
Section One: The Sacramental Economy

Commentary 17: Christ's Presence in the Liturgy, and Our Faith

Q. How does the *Catechism* treat the way we worship?

A. Part two, "The Celebration of the Christian Mystery," covers that topic at length (#1066–690), although it is shorter than part one, which deals with our beliefs. There are two sections in this treatment: "The Sacramental Economy" and "The Seven Sacraments of the Church."

Q. What does the phrase "sacramental economy" mean?

A. What Christ did in the Holy Land two thousand years ago, he continues to accomplish today in and with his Church. Jesus does this by acting through the sacraments. By sacramental liturgies, Christ communicates, or dispenses, to us the fruits of his coming, dying, and rising—his paschal, or Easter, mystery. The common tradition of the East and West calls that process of communication or dispensation of the Lord's graces "the sacramental economy."

Q. Why do we use the word "bless" or "blessings" at every Mass?

A. A blessing can be either a gift we have received from our God on high or the praise we offer to the Creator and Savior for the gift received. Our biblical, liturgical, and theological tradition maintains that everything we possess is a gift from God. Consequently, our worship always includes themes of praise and thanks.

For example, the Hebrew word *berakah*, which we use during the presentation of gifts ("Blessed are you, Lord, God of creation..."), could be translated in this way: "We praise, adore, and surrender to you, our Creator, in thanksgiving for your gifts."

Q. Do the sacraments always work?

A. If the sacraments are celebrated according to the Church's intention and the recipients have the proper dispositions, the sacraments always work—that is, they bestow or confer the grace they signify. They do not depend totally upon the personal holiness of the celebrant. However, the faith and fervor of both the celebrant and the recipient determine the fruits of the sacrament or the degree of their effectiveness.

Q. Isn't this almost magical?

A. Perhaps. But the sacraments' effectiveness depends upon the fact that Christ himself is at work in them. It is he who baptizes, forgives, anoints. It is the power of Jesus and his Spirit acting in and through the sacramental rituals that makes them efficacious.

Q. Where can we find the Church's teaching on this unique presence of Christ in our worship?

A. The most current and succinct expression of that concept occurs in the *Constitution on the Sacred Liturgy* from the Second Vatican Council. The *Catechism* excerpts from article 7 an entire paragraph clearly communicating this notion of Christ's presence. That teaching serves as the theological basis for the liturgical changes over the past three decades.

"Christ is always present in his Church, especially in her liturgical celebrations," the text reads (#1088). It goes on to list the various ways in which Jesus is present: in the Eucharist, the sacraments, the Word, and in the assembly when the Church prays and sings.

Q. How does faith fit into this picture?

A. The sacraments presuppose, demand, or require faith if they are to bear fruit. However, by words and objects they also nourish, strengthen, and express faith.

Recommended Reading

Articles 1066–162.

Commentary 18: The Liturgical Year

Q. Why was an older book called *The Church's Year of Grace?*

A. Father Pius Parsch wrote this several volume text before the Second Vatican Council to describe the riches connected with the Church's liturgical year. That annual celebration of feasts has a double dimension. One series centers around the mysteries of Christ (for example, Christmas and Easter); the other focuses on those people who with great determination during their lives on earth sought to imitate Jesus as perfectly as possible—the saints (for example, St. Peter and St. Maria Goretti). The Church teaches that there are unique graces or blessings to be gained by celebrating with faith any of these liturgies.

Q. What is the reason for keeping the Sabbath, really Saturday, on Sunday?

A. Our Lord rose from the dead on Easter Sunday and, with the Father, sent the Holy Spirit fifty days later on Pentecost, also a Sunday. For Catholics, therefore, Sunday is primarily a day honoring the risen Jesus. It also, however, as the first day of the week, recalls the first day of creation. Moreover, as the eighth day, it recollects how Christ after his Holy Saturday Sabbath rest inaugurated the "day the Lord has made" by his rising from the dead. Pagans of those early centuries did have a "day of the sun" celebration; Christians thus then began to have their own "day of the Son," the Savior Son who dispels darkness by his light.

Q. Which is the more significant feast, Christmas or Easter?

A. Easter. It was the first and only celebration in the beginning; today we call Easter the "Feast of Feasts" or the "Solemnity of Solemnities." Over the centuries, the Church has developed a marvelous array of other feasts that lead to or flow from Easter. We group a number of these major celebrations into two main cycles, each with a preparation and a prolongation period. Advent leads us to Christmas; we then rejoice over the Lord's coming for several weeks of a Christmas season, which concludes with Epiphany and the Baptism of the Lord. Lent prepares us for Easter; we prolong that for fifty days of an Easter season until Pentecost.

Q. Will there ever be an end to changes in the liturgy?

A. Not totally. We have experienced a massive renewal and reform of Catholic worship over the past thirty years. Further ritual changes in the immediate future will likely be relatively few in number and minor in nature. Still, the bishops of the Second Vatican Council and Pope John Paul II, as well as the new *Catechism,* which cites both of these sources, remind us that the liturgy has two parts: a divinely instituted, immutable, or unchangeable, element, and human changeable features. The Church can, has, and must at times modify these latter parts for the good of its people. The shift in the regulations for eucharistic fasting during the 1960s is a practical illustration of such a change.

Q. How does the *Catechism* treat the seven sacraments?

A. Its very division of them into three distinct sections communicates some truths about these rites. The sacraments of Christian initiation are baptism, confirmation, and the Eucharist. The sacraments of healing are penance, or reconciliation, and the anointing of the sick. The sacraments at the service of communion are holy orders and matrimony.

Recommended Reading

Articles 1163–255.

Section Two: The Seven Sacraments of the Church

Commentary 19: Baptism and Confirmation

Q. Are priests the only persons who can and may baptize?

A. No. An official function of deacons is to baptize. Moreover, in emergencies any person, including those not Catholic or not even baptized, can and may baptize. This situation most often occurs at hospitals with regard to seriously ailing infants. In such circumstances, attending healthcare personnel may baptize when the priest or deacon chaplain is not available.

Q. Is baptism necessary for our salvation?

A. Yes. Jesus indicated so in John's Gospel (3:5). But those who seek the truth and do the will of God in accordance with their understanding of it can be saved. These people have a baptism of desire—they would opt for this sacrament if they knew its necessity.

Q. What about infants who die without baptism?

A. The *Catechism* makes no mention of "limbo," a theory once used to explain the fate of children who die without baptism. Instead, it entrusts these little ones to the mercy and love of God. The Church does so with a confidence based on the Bible. The Scriptures tell us that Jesus came to save all; they also describe his love for children, how he embraced and blessed them. Still, the *Catechism* urges that infants be baptized relatively soon after birth.

Q. Does a bishop always confirm?

A. No. A priest can confirm if a person is near death and the bishop is not nearby; when an adult enters the Church, as at the Easter Vigil; and if specially delegated to do so by the bishop.

Q. Why does the Eastern, or Oriental, Catholic Church (for example, Ukrainian Catholics) follow a different practice for confirmation?

A. Confirmation has two fundamental functions: to strengthen or complete (confirm) the baptized person, and to forge a closer bond with other Catholic Christians through the bishop. Eastern churches emphasize the former by having the priest confirm immediately after and as part of the infant's baptism. Western, or Latin-rite, churches stress the latter by having the bishop confirm candidates at a later date after they reach the age of reason. Both, however, reflect a connection with others through the bishop by using for the sacrament perfumed oil or chrism blessed by the bishop and distributed to all the parishes.

Q. When are young people confirmed?

A. Today it varies from area to area. Most dioceses have delayed confirmation to adolescence, preceded by a two-year preparation program of study, prayer, and service. However, a growing trend seems to be developing that places confirmation just before first Communion. That preserves or resurrects the ancient tradition of baptism, confirmation, and Eucharist.

Q. Is confirmation necessary for salvation or for marriage?

A. No. But it is highly desirable for all Catholics to receive this sacrament as a help toward their salvation and prior to matrimony.

Recommended Reading

Articles 1256–344.

Commentary 20: The Eucharist

Q. Does the Church hold the Eucharist in special regard?

A. Yes. It terms the Eucharist as the summit and source of the Church's life. It calls this *the* sacrament. It sees all the other sacraments as leading to and flowing from the Eucharist. For those reasons, Church leaders grew justly alarmed when a recent American survey indicated a surprisingly high percentage of contemporary Catholics lacked a firm belief in Christ's eucharistic presence.

Q. Where do we first find a description of the Mass in the early Christian centuries?

A. Around the year 155, St. Justin the Martyr wrote to a pagan emperor and described the basic pattern of eucharistic celebrations. That format has remained essentially the same to the present time, even though there have been incidental yet significant changes at different places and in different periods. For example, according to Justin's account, the sign of peace occurred after the general intercessions or the Prayer of the Faithful, rather than in its current location, following the Our Father and before Communion.

Q. What happened to the notion that there are three principal parts of Mass: offertory, consecration, and Communion?

A. They remain, of course, but the Church today proposes a different overall view of the Mass, one that better mirrors the description of St. Justin. This notion divides Eucharistic celebrations into two parts: the first centers around the pulpit, or lectern, and the Bible, the Word of God; the second centers around the altar and the body and blood of Christ. These two parts are termed the Liturgy of the Word and the Liturgy of the Eucharist.

Q. How does this Liturgy of the Word flow?

A. It contains a gathering and then the Liturgy of the Word proper with readings, homily, and general intercessions.

Q. And the Liturgy of the Eucharist?

A. It contains the presentation of the bread and wine, the consecratory thanksgiving, Communion, and a dismissal.

Q. Why do we always have a collection at Mass?

A. It reassures visitors that they are in a Catholic Church. Seriously, the collection obviously provides needed funds but more importantly carries out an ancient tradition. The *Catechism* states: "From the very beginning Christians have brought, along with bread and wine for the Eucharist, gifts to share with those in need. This custom of the *collection*, ever appropriate, is inspired by the example of Christ who became poor to make us rich" (#1351).

Q. Can we ever fully understand the Eucharist?

A. No. It is a mystery, but by examining this mystery from several perspectives we come to grasp more fully the richness of the Eucharist. The Church thus sees the Eucharist as thanksgiving and praise to the Father, the sacrificial memorial of Christ and his Body, and the presence of Jesus brought about by the power of the Holy Spirit.

Q. Is Christ really present in the Eucharist?

A. Yes. The Church officially declares that *"the whole Christ is truly, really and substantially* contained" under the Eucharistic species of bread and wine (#1374). For that reason, it surrounds eucharistic worship with symbols (like candles and vestments) and gestures (like genuflecting and bowing deeply) to deepen faith and express reverence before this Presence.

Q. Does the Church still urge prayer before the tabernacle?

A. The Church strongly recommends our adoration of the Lord in the Eucharist not only during Mass but outside of it, "reserving the consecrated hosts with the utmost care, exposing them to the solemn veneration of the faithful, and carrying them in procession" (#1378–81).

Recommended Reading

Articles 1345–419.

*Commentary 21: The First Healing Sacrament—
Penance, or Reconciliation*

Q. What are the sacraments of healing?

A. During his life on earth Jesus forgave the paralytic and cured his ailment. Christ thus healed him spiritually and physically. The Lord continues to heal today, especially through the two "healing" sacraments: penance, or reconciliation; and anointing of the sick.

Q. Is "confession" still part of Catholic life?

A. The practice is, but the term "confession" now has generally been replaced by penance or reconciliation. "Confession" does not fully or adequately describe the sacrament that forgives sins. We do confess our sins as part of the ritual, but there are additional and even more crucial elements. These include, for example, conversion of heart, faith in God's mercy, satisfaction for misdeeds, and reform of our lives.

Q. Does not "penance" refer to Lenten sacrifices or the prayers we recite after confession?

A. Yes. However, when we speak about the sacrament of penance, the word means more than those two items. It does signify the change of heart needed for forgiveness and penitential acts like Lenten sacrifices, but also refers to those steps of the official rite that we follow to achieve that inner healing.

Q. Why does the Church now also call this sacrament "reconciliation"?

A. Sin weakens or breaks several of our relationships: with God, others, the world around us, and our inner selves. Consequently, to be healed spiritually and forgiven totally requires a reconciling of all those relationships.

Q. Do Catholics have to go to confession?

A. Church law requires Catholic adults to confess serious sins at least once a year. There is also an obligation to receive Communion at least once a year during the Easter season (a period extended by the Church from Ash Wednesday through Trinity Sunday). We often in the past, therefore, spoke about making one's Easter duty, a task that usually included both confession and Communion. However, note that the obligation to confess pertains only to serious sins.

Q. Must we confess if there are no serious sins?

A. Strictly and legally speaking—no. Nevertheless, the Church strongly encourages Catholics to receive the sacrament of penance often, even when there are but everyday faults (venial sins) to confess. In the words of the *Catechism,* regular confession of such lesser moral failures "helps us form our conscience, fight against evil tendencies, let ourselves be healed by Christ and progress in the life of the Spirit" (#1458).

Q. Are children required to receive this sacrament before their first holy Communion?

A. The *Catechism,* echoing Canon 914 in the new Code of Canon Law, states, "Children must go to the sacrament of Penance before receiving Holy Communion for the first time" (#1457). My book *With Hearts Light as Feathers* discusses the sacrament of reconciliation for children and treats this particular question in depth.

Q. May a priest ever reveal sins confessed to him in this sacrament?

A. No, not ever, not under any circumstances. Again, referring to the Code of Canon Law, the *Catechism* declares that "every priest who hears confessions is bound under very severe penalties to keep absolute secrecy regarding the sins that his penitents have confessed to him." This secrecy, it goes on to say, "admits of no exceptions" (#1467).

Recommended Reading

Articles 1420–98.

Commentary 22: The Second Healing Sacrament— Anointing of the Sick

Q. Where did the phrase "the last rites" originate?

A. An obvious answer is the fact that most often in the past priests ministered these rituals to people near death. This phenomenon in itself frequently led Catholics to postpone calling the clergy for seriously sick relatives. A priest's presence seemingly meant the end was imminent and might further frighten the ailing individual.

However, there is a more technical answer.

The Church in pre–Vatican II days termed this sacrament "extreme unction"— that is, the last or final anointing. Last or final, not so much as the last or final before death, but the last or final of the anointings with oil that Catholics receive during their lives. Thus, we begin with the oil of the catechumens at baptism, continue with the chrism of confirmation, and now, in serious illness, conclude with the oil of the sick.

Q. What is the proper term today?

A. When the revised rite appeared about twenty-five years ago, our Church renamed this ritual the sacrament for the "anointing of the sick." It thereby shifted the emphasis to more of a "healing" function rather than a death-preparation event. Catholics who understand this change in thrust are now less reluctant to summon the clergy for critically ill individuals.

Q. How does this healing sacrament help?

A. Anointing of the sick has several healing effects: it helps the sick person bravely bear the difficulties that go with a serious illness or the frailty of old age, by providing strength, peace, and courage; it supplies inner assistance for warding off temptations to discouragement and eases anguish in the face of death; it leads to a healing of the soul and also of the body, "if such is God's will"; finally, it forgives any sins that have been committed.

Q. Who may receive the sacrament?

A. Anyone who is dangerously sick, suffering from a grave illness, or in danger of death from sickness or old age. This means a person must be suffering from more than a heavy cold but, on the other hand, need not be close to death's door to receive the sacrament.

The Church encourages those who face a serious operation to receive this sacrament. It also recommends anointing those elderly persons whose failing has become more pronounced.

Persons who have recovered and then slip back into a seriously sick state may be anointed again.

Q. Is there a biblical basis for the anointing of the sick?

A. The Church declares that the sacrament was instituted by Christ as one of the sacraments. Biblically speaking, we see the sacrament alluded to in Mark's Gospel (Mark 6:13) and promulgated or officially proclaimed by James the Apostle (James 5:14–15).

Q. Are priests and bishops the only persons to minister this sacrament to the sick?

A. Yes. However, the Church recognizes that some people other than priests or bishops possess a special charism, grace, or power to heal. We have seen that more general healing ministry emerge strongly in the last two decades.

Jesus' words in Mark 16:17–18 lend support to such efforts. As related there, the Lord promised that those who in Christ's name lay hands upon the sick will see them recover.

Recommended Reading

Articles 1499–532.

Commentary 23: Sacraments at the Service of Communion— Holy Orders

Q. Where are we now?

A. Having covered the three initiation sacraments (baptism, confirmation, and Eucharist) and the two healing sacraments (penance and anointing of the sick), we now take up the two other sacraments, those at the service of communion: holy orders and matrimony.

Q. Why this new concept, "at the service of communion"?

A. Holy orders and matrimony are directed toward saving others or contributing to their salvation. If these sacraments help the ordained or married person grow in personal holiness and draw closer to salvation, it is precisely through service to others that they do so.

Q. What does the term "holy orders" mean?

A. In ancient Roman days, the word *order* designated a body of persons, especially a governing body of individuals. Ordination meant the process by which one became a member of a particular order. In time, the Church used the phrase "holy orders" to designate more specifically the orders or bodies of bishops, priests, and deacons. Ordination became a religious and liturgical act, a blessing, consecration, or sacrament, which incorporated a person into one of those orders. It also bestowed upon that individual the sacred power needed to carry out the connected duties.

Q. Does the notion of priesthood have roots in the past?

A. The Church sees in the Old Testament priesthoods (Aaron, Levites, the seventy elders) a type or prefigurement of the New Testament priesthood. However, Christ is the one mediator between God and us. Jesus is the only true priest; all others are but his ministers.

Q. Will ordination guarantee holiness in a bishop, priest, or deacon?

A. No. Even though the ordained person acts with the power and in the place of Christ, that does not mean this individual is preserved from human weaknesses, from a spirit of domination, from error, or from sin. The sacraments communicate grace regardless of the minister's worthiness, but the ordained person's faults can diminish the effectiveness of those rituals and likewise wound the Church.

Q. How are bishops, priests, and deacons ordained?

A. The bishop's task is to sanctify, teach, and rule. Ordination bestows upon the candidate the fullness of holy orders and brings him into the college of bishops.

For that reason, several bishops, according to an ancient tradition, must participate in the ordination of a new bishop.

A priest's task, as co-worker with the bishop, is to preach the gospel, shepherd the faithful, and celebrate divine worship. Ordination bestows upon the candidate the powers needed for those tasks and also inserts him into an intimate brotherhood with other priests. For that reason, a bishop ordains to the priesthood, assisted by the priests present who lay hands upon the candidate(s).

A deacon's task is to serve the bishop and priests in a variety of liturgical ways and through diverse ministries of charity. The bishop ordains the deacon candidates, but any priests present do not lay hands on their heads.

In all three cases, the essential rite is the laying on of hands by the bishop and a special consecratory prayer.

Q. Is ordination to the priesthood limited to men?

A. Yes. Not surprisingly, the *Catechism* echoes the recent declaration of Pope John Paul II on this subject. It explains that since Christ chose men to form the college of apostles and they did the same when they selected collaborators in this ministry, the Church sees itself bound by the choice the Lord made. For this reason, the *Catechism* states, ordination of women is not possible.

Recommended Reading

Articles 1533–600.

Commentary 24: Sacraments at the Service of Communion— Matrimony

Q. Is marriage from God or of purely human origin?

A. The Church views marriage as divinely instituted and cites the Genesis story about Adam and Eve in support of this position. God commands a man and a woman to leave parents, marry, and become no longer two but one flesh. The Church maintains that Jesus subsequently elevated the natural state of marriage to the level of a sacrament.

Q. Who ministers the sacrament of matrimony?

A. In the Latin, or Western, rite of the Church, clergy or specially delegated individuals witness the vows, but the couple themselves minister this sacrament to one another as they exchange permanent promises. In the Eastern rites of our Church, the bishop or priest ministers the sacrament, successively "crowning" the bridegroom and bride as a sign of their marriage bond.

Q. What are the effects of this sacrament?

A. The Risen Lord becomes present in a special way as two people exchange vows that bind them together for life. But Jesus remains with them for the rest of their lives as well. Christ assures the new husband and wife that in their future he will provide them with all the wisdom and strength they will need to lead a Christian married life.

Q. For a couple to be married in the Church, is it required that they regularly attend Mass, participate in reconciliation, and receive Communion?

A. Ideally, yes. Those are necessary for a couple to reap the sacrament's full benefits. However, the only essential requirements are that at least one be a baptized Catholic and that both wish to marry according to the mind of God, that is, to commit themselves perpetually and exclusively to one another.

Q. Are there special arrangements for a Catholic marrying one who is not Catholic?

A. In the United States, the Church provides great flexibility in these often delicate situations. There must be an understanding that the Catholic partner will do her or his best to have the children baptized and reared as Catholics. However, the person who is not Catholic need not sign or make any promises in this regard. Moreover, the couples have the freedom to select pretty much the type and location of a wedding ceremony that best fits their circumstances.

Q. How does the Church deal with divorce?

A. Following the teaching of Jesus as articulated in Mark's Gospel, the Church opposes divorce. Marriage is for better or worse, until death parts the pair. But the Church also recognizes, particularly in these turbulent times, that the marriages of some couples, now legally separated or divorced, were fatally flawed from the start. In those situations, the Church conducts a quite thorough but still reasonably brief examination of the marriage in question. If the facts warrant the decision, it issues a declaration of nullity. That statement does not negate the fact of the marriage or the legitimacy of the children, but declares that it was never the kind of sacramental bond that only death can break asunder.

Q. Does the Church offer good marriage preparation programs?

A. Excellent ones on both the parish, regional, and diocesan level. It is accurate to say that today no couple marries in the Church without experiencing some kind of quality informational and inspirational premarital program.

Recommended Reading

Articles 1601–66.

Commentary 25: Sacramentals, Devotions, Funerals

Q. What are sacramentals?

A. They are sacred signs that resemble the sacraments but differ from them in number, types, and power. There are only seven sacraments but an almost unlimited number of sacramentals. The sacraments pertain to a few major moments and occasions in life; the sacramentals touch almost every aspect of human existence. The sacraments possess a power from Christ to communicate grace by themselves; the effectiveness of sacramentals depends upon the prayer of the Church and the faith or devotion of those using them.

Q. Would you clarify this by examples?

A. A home, car, and children's college tuition are probably three of any family's most significant investments. *The Book of Blessings,* prepared for use in the United States, contains sacramental rites designed to bring those significant outlays into the sphere of formal prayer and worship. It contains, for example, a blessing for vehicles, for houses, and for teachers or students. These blessings can be ministered by the clergy, of course, but laypersons can also preside over them. Their effectiveness, however, will only be in proportion to the devotion of the participants.

The Book of Blessings provides a remarkably rich, extensive, and diversified collection of such rituals. These include blessings for many and varied items, like an engaged couple, a flag, domestic pets, or seeds for spring planting.

Q. Does the Church still employ exorcisms?

A. Yes. A simple exorcism forms part of every baptismal ceremony. But major or solemn exorcisms can be performed only by a priest with the explicit permission of the bishop and are to be executed rarely and with extreme caution.

Q. Are there guidelines for popular devotions?

A. The Church encourages them but stresses that they should harmonize with the liturgical season and flow from or lead to official worship. For example, Christmas carols during Advent weaken the celebration of that "waiting" or preparation season. Emphasis in word or song on Christ's passion during the first part of Lent runs contrary to the motif of those weeks, which centers instead around baptism and renewal; Jesus' suffering and death emerge more centrally in the latter part of the Lenten season.

Q. How important are the readings and homily at a funeral service?

A. Extremely. The *Catechism* mentions that the Liturgy of the Word at funerals demands very careful preparation because there are often present Catholics who rarely attend the liturgy and friends of the deceased or bereaved who are not Christians. These are thus significant occasions for evangelization.

Q. Where are we heading now in our discussion?

A. We have completed part two, "The Celebration of the Christian Mystery" (#1066–690). We now begin part three, "Life in Christ." It is rather lengthy (190 pages, articles 1691–2557) and contains two sections. The first one treats our vocation, which is "life in the Spirit." The second one examines the Ten Commandments.

Q. Is this part practical?

A. Very much so, although it begins with lofty and basic notions. These concepts, however, are the foundation for its highly specific application to contemporary moral issues, like animal rights, the death penalty, and business ethics.

Recommended Reading

Articles 1667–90.

PART THREE: LIFE IN CHRIST
Section One: [Our] Vocation: Life in the Spirit

Commentary 26: General Moral Principles

Q. Doesn't Pope John Paul II speak often about the dignity of the human person?

A. Yes. Underscoring all of his many writings and countless talks is this notion about the dignity of the human person. We see that concept reflected in the new *Catechism,* which contains an entire chapter of 187 articles, or 34 pages, dedicated to the subject.

Q. What is the basis for this dignity?

A. The foundation and essential source of human dignity rests upon the fact that we have been created in the image and likeness of God. As a result of that unique creation, every person possesses, among other gifts, a spiritual and immortal soul, a reason capable of understanding, a free will able to choose good or evil, the divine inner presence, and a destiny of perfect and permanent happiness.

Q. Why are so many people unhappy in this life?

A. We cannot give a simple answer to that question. However, while there are many joys and pleasures here on earth, the final fulfillment of all happiness awaits us in the life to come. Two great saints have placed this yearning in context. St.

Augustine said, "Our hearts are restless and will not rest until they rest in God." Centuries later, St. Thomas stated, "God alone satisfies."

Q. Does the *Catechism* deal specifically with the practical moral challenges facing us today?

A. The second section of "Life in Christ" addresses an amazing number of particular morality issues like ecology, euthanasia, and gambling. But it initially establishes more general principles for determining the rightness and wrongness of human actions. That first section covers what older courses in the seminary termed fundamental moral theology.

Q. Could you illustrate some of those generic norms?

A. Here are several subjects treated and an example of a connected practical conclusion or consequence for each topic:

- Freedom—We are free to choose between good and evil, but "the more one does what is good, the freer one becomes" (#1733).
- Responsibility—We are responsible for our own freely chosen actions, although that responsibility can be diminished or eliminated by "ignorance, inadvertence, duress, fear, habit, inordinate attachments, and other psychological or social factors" (#1735).
- Objective moral laws—"There are acts which, in and of themselves, independently of circumstances and intentions, are always gravely illicit by reason of their object; such as blasphemy and perjury, murder and adultery" (#1756).
- Conscience—This "is a judgment of reason whereby [human persons recognize] the moral quality of a concrete act that [they are] going to perform, [are] in the process of performing or [have] already completed" (#1778).
- Sacredness of Conscience—"Conscience is [our] most secret core and [our] sanctuary. There [we are] alone with God whose voice echoes in [our] depths" (#1776). "[We] must always obey the certain judgment of [our] conscience" (#1790).

Q. Do we have help in making right choices?

A. Yes. We have available for us virtues, human and divine, or natural and supernatural, which are firm and habitual dispositions to do good. These include the cardinal virtues of prudence, justice, fortitude and temperance; the theological virtues of faith, hope, and charity; the gifts of the Holy Spirit.

Recommended Reading

Articles 1691–845.

Commentary 27: Sin

Q. What is the difference between mortal and venial sin?

A. Sin occurs when we disregard the divine imperative within us, disobey our conscience, or fail to follow God's voice in our heart, which says, "Do this" or "Don't do that."

When that disregard, disobedience, or failure involves a grave or serious matter, we term it a mortal sin. This word *mortal,* from its Latin roots, means "death-dealing" because it breaks our relationship with the Lord, drives the life of grace from our hearts here on earth, and, without repentance, would deprive us of the life of glory in heaven.

When that disregard, disobedience, or failure involves a lesser matter, or our culpability is diminished because of various factors, we term it a venial sin. The word *venial* indicates that it is less serious and more easily forgiven and that it weakens but does not rupture our relationship with the Lord.

Q. How do we commit a mortal sin?

A. Three conditions must be fulfilled at once: grave or serious matter, full knowledge of what we are doing, and free or complete consent to this action.

As we mentioned in an earlier question, murder and adultery are examples of a seriously or gravely wrong act. However, not knowing the other person is married would eliminate the adultery evil of the action, although the seriously wrong fornication dimension would still exist. Moreover, passion, external pressures, or pathological disorders could diminish the voluntary, or free, character of the action. In such a case, the action itself would be grave or serious matter, but the subjective sin would be less (or none at all) because of the defective consent.

Q. Who determines if a sin is mortal or not?

A. Only God. Human beings can judge that an act in itself is seriously wrong, but judgments about the person who carried out the action must be left to God's justice and mercy.

Q. How do we commit a venial sin?

A. We commit a venial sin when the matter is less serious or, if it is serious, we act without full knowledge or complete consent. Lying, for example, is always wrong, but not necessarily as serious a wrong as adultery. Moreover, if through no fault of our own we did not know some act was gravely wrong or did not fully "give in" to the evil action or temptation, this would be a venial sin.

Q. Are there sins that God will never forgive?

A. Only the sin or unwillingness to repent of disbelief in God's mercy. The biblical warning about the sin against the Holy Spirit that can never be forgiven is precisely that—refusal to repent and rejection of divine forgiveness.

Q. Is sin individual and personal or social and communal?

A. Both. All sin is personal. But personal sins can give rise to situations, structures, and institutions that run contrary to God's plan and harm others. Consequently, we also call those structures sinful and those sins social.

Q. Must we always obey civil laws?

A. Society and its laws should be based upon the transcendent dignity of the human person and the essential equality of each individual. Structures that fail to uphold those qualities may and even must be disobeyed.

Recommended Reading

Articles 1846–948.

Commentary 28: Salvation, Law, and Grace

Q. How does God help us reach our ultimate goal—the perfect happiness of heaven?

A. Salvation is only from the Lord. We cannot earn or win an eternal reward by our own efforts alone. But divine assistance comes to our rescue in Christ the Savior through the moral law that guides us and God's grace that sustains us.

Q. What is this moral law?

A. There are several, actually, although all have their sources in God's eternal law: the natural law written in the human heart; laws divinely revealed through the pages of the Old or New Testament; Church laws; and civil laws.

Q. Isn't *natural law* an outdated concept?

A. We term this law "natural" because it is based upon human nature, that is, it resides within human beings who possess reason and will. Centuries ago, St. Thomas Aquinas described natural law in these words:

> *The natural law is nothing other than the light of understanding placed in us by God; through it we know what we must do and what we must avoid. God has given this light or law at the creation.*

Our human nature has not changed, but because of environmental and cultural factors, we often do not perceive clearly and immediately what the natural law tells us. Such would be the case today and part of the reason for Pope John Paul II's recent encyclical *The Gospel of Life,* which calls on us to reaffirm life in our current "culture of death."

Q. Are there different kinds of graces?

A. Yes. The word itself means "gift." Grace is a favor from the Creator, the free and undeserved help that God gives us to follow moral laws and achieve our eternal goal. This assistance comes in various ways.

Through sanctifying or deifying grace, the Holy Trinity, including the Risen Christ, dwells within us. Through actual graces, God gives us, on specific occasions, light and strength to follow the divine plan. Through sacramental graces, the Lord provides special gifts enabling us to carry out the purpose of each sacrament. Through graces of state, God helps us carry out the personal responsibilities that we bear in the Church or the world.

Q. Is the pope infallible, and must we obey him?

A. The Holy Father is indeed infallible, but only on matters of faith or morals and when speaking formally as head of the Church in union with bishops throughout the world. There have been very few instances of infallible proclamations over the past 150 years. However, even when he is not speaking infallibly, his teachings deserve our docility, attention, openness, and even obedience.

Q. What are some major precepts, or laws, of the Church?

A.   1. "You shall attend Mass on Sundays and holy days of obligation."
   2. "You should confess your sins at least once a year."
   3. "You should humbly receive your Creator in Holy Communion at least once during the Easter season."
   4. "You should observe the prescribed days of fast and abstinence."

Recommended Reading

Articles 1949–2051.

Section Two: The Ten Commandments

Commentary 29: Ten Commandments

Q. How are we doing?

A. You have finished about 70 percent of the *Catechism*. That means you've studied nearly five hundred pages and over two thousand articles. We have also just completed section one of part three, "Life in Christ." That section deals with our human vocation, our "life in the Spirit," and examines general principles of morality. Now we move to section two of part three, which treats the Ten Commandments. Using the Decalogue for a framework, it touches upon a host of specific contemporary moral issues.

Q. Where did we discover the Ten Commandments?

A. In our hearts and through God's revelation written down in the Bible. Centuries ago, St. Irenaeus said, "From the beginning, God had implanted in the heart of man precepts of the natural law. Then he was content to remind him of them. This was the Decalogue."

Human reason alone could have arrived at the Ten Commandments. However, because of our flawed nature, we no longer clearly perceived those rules nor completely understood them. St. Bonaventure noted this: "A full explanation of the commandments of the Decalogue became necessary in the state of sin because the light of reason was obscured and the will had gone astray."

Q. What sections of the Bible contain the Decalogue?

A. Prior to section two of part three, the *Catechism* provides an interesting table that lists the Ten Commandments as found in the book of Exodus (20:2–17), in the book of Deuteronomy (5:6–21), and in a traditional catechetical formula.

Q. Are the Ten Commandments also called the Decalogue?

A. Yes. The term *Decalogue* means literally "ten words." God revealed these "ten words" to Moses and through him to the Chosen People on the holy mountain. They were written not by Moses but by the "finger of God." Other Old Testament books refer to these "ten words" (Hosea, Jeremiah, Ezekiel), but only in the New Covenant or Testament with Jesus Christ is the full meaning of the Decalogue revealed.

Q. Why do we connect the covenant with the commandments?

A. The Decalogue is God's rule of life for us and our response to the Creator's loving and liberating action on our behalf. This love and liberation displayed itself in the divine action that freed the Chosen People from slavery in Egypt. These "ten words" that God subsequently wrote on two tables of stone and gave to Moses were

God's law for right living and, at the same time, the proper response of human beings to the Lord who initiated this loving exchange. These "tables of the testimony" were later deposited in the ark of the covenant.

Q. Is there a personal tone to the commandments?

A. Yes. The obligations of the commandments are stated in the first person ("I am the Lord") and addressed to another person ("You" shall not...). God thus makes known the divine will to people as individuals.

Q. Who determined the order of the Decalogue?

A. The division and numbering of the Ten Commandments have varied over the years. The *Catechism* follows the order established by St. Augustine, traditional in the Catholic Church, and also observed by Lutheran churches. The early Greek religious leaders developed a slightly different order, one now followed by Orthodox churches and reformed worshiping communities.

Q. What is that order in the *Catechism*?

A. It is based upon Jesus' declaration of the two great commandments: loving God and our neighbor. The first three commandments refer to our dealings with God; the next seven refer to the way we should relate to our neighbors.

Recommended Reading

Articles 2052–82.

Commentary 30: The First and Second Commandments

Q. What is the meaning of the first commandment?

A. There are four components to the first commandment: first, to worship the Lord our God; second, to serve only God; third, to have no other gods besides the true God; and fourth, to make no graven images.

Q. Are all the commandments negative?

A. Many are expressed in negative terms, but each of them has a positive dimension. For example, "You shall not kill" also implies that we show care and concern for all creatures.

Q. How do we worship the Lord our God?

A. Through faith, hope, and love.
Faith means to believe in God who is a constant, unchangeable being, always the same, loyal and just, without any evil. Voluntary doubts, heresy, apostasy, and

schism are some ways in which we can fail in this regard. However, difficulties in believing are not the same as doubts. Difficulties are really struggles or temptations; only true doubting would be sinful.

Hope requires that we trust God will give us the capacity to love the Lord in return and live a life of love. Despair and presumption are twin tests against hope.

Love requires that we in fact love God above everything and all creatures for and because of God.

Q. How do we serve only God?

A. By adoration, prayer, sacrifice, promises, vows, and evangelical counsels of poverty, chastity, and obedience.

The counsels, however ideal, are not an obligation for anyone. In the course of Church history there have always been some too intense people who have tried to make these invitations of Christ to be poor, chaste, and obedient into a command from the Lord.

Occasionally, individuals make promises or vows to God under pressure. The Church can in certain circumstances dispense from such vows or promises.

Q. How do we have no other gods besides the true God?

A. By avoiding superstition, idolatry, magic, religious inactivity, disbelief in God, or doubt of the Lord.

In most of these situations, we would be placing our hearts and trust in creatures rather than in God. Idolatry, for example, may occur when our top priority actually centers in reality around power, pleasure, money, work, and so on.

Curiosity about or association with the occult or Satan, even if in a joking, half-hearted manner, are unhealthy and risky practices.

Q. How do we avoid making graven images?

A. Both in the Old Testament and early Church worship, material images have been used to help us pray. The bronze serpent and the ark of the covenant as well as representations of Christ and Mary are illustrations of that ancient tradition.

St. Thomas Aquinas explained the appropriate use of images as opposed to the worship of them:

> *Religious worship is not directed to images in themselves, considered as mere things, but under their distinctive aspect as images leading us on to God incarnate. The movement toward the image does not terminate in it as image, but tends towards that whose image it is.*

Q. What is the meaning of the second commandment?

A. To recognize that God's name is holy, that this name should not be taken in vain, and that every person's name, especially a Christian's name, is unique and special.

Using God's or Jesus' name reverently in prayer or irreverently in anger are obvious instances of obeying or disobeying this commandment.

Recommended Reading

Articles 2083–167.

Commentary 31: The Third and Fourth Commandments

Q. What is the meaning of the word *sabbath* in the third commandment?

A. "Remember to keep holy the sabbath day" means, literally, to keep holy Saturday, the seventh day of the week. Faithful Jewish people today observe the sabbath from sundown Friday to sundown Saturday.

The sabbath has rich connections with events in the Old Testament or Hebrew Scriptures. It recalls the creation of the world. It recalls the deliverance of the Chosen People from pagan slavery in Egypt and the obligation of the liberated ones to remember that divine intervention on the sabbath day. It recalls the covenant that God made with us as we observe a day of praise and gratitude for the Lord's saving actions. It recalls the fact that God rested on the seventh day as a model for us to imitate.

Q. Why, then, do most Christians keep the sabbath on Sunday?

A. At the very beginning of the Christian era, the Church shifted this observance from Saturday to Sunday, basically for two reasons: Jesus rose on Easter Sunday, and the Holy Spirit came upon the apostles fifty days later, also a Sunday. It also sees in this celebration an understanding that Christ ushered in the new creation and fulfills the sabbath.

Q. Is Mass central to keeping Sunday holy?

A. Yes. There is a double dimension to the Sunday obligation—praising our God and resting from work. The Church, also from ancient times, has stated that the "Sunday celebration of the Lord's Day and his Eucharist is at the heart of the Church's life" (#2177). Sunday is *the* feast day, the foremost holy day of obligation, and was for years the only celebration of the Church year. Every Sunday, therefore, is a little Easter.

Q. Do Catholics have an obligation to be present for Mass every Sunday?

A. Yes, or at an anticipated Mass on Saturday evening. Over the past thirty years, there has been some unclear teaching about the serious responsibility of Catholics to attend Sunday Mass each week and a generally lax approach among many Catholics in that regard. The *Catechism* gives clear teaching on this topic.

The Sunday Eucharist is the foundation and confirmation of all Christian practice. For this reason the faithful are obliged to participate in the Eucharist on days of obligation, unless excused for a serious reason (for example, illness, the care of infants) or dispensed by their own pastor. Those who deliberately fail in this obligation commit a grave sin (#2181).

Q. How do we observe Sunday as a day of rest?

A. By avoiding unnecessary work and engaging in activities that will "recreate" us and all those with whom we are connected.

Q. Which is the most important of the commandments?

A. The greatest commandment is not one found in the Decalogue, but an injunction beyond all ten: To love God with our whole heart and our neighbor as ourself. Commandments 1–3 deal with the first part of that assertion; commandments 4–10 spell out the meaning of the second part.

Q. Who are my "father and mother"?

A. This commandment to honor our parents also includes the responsibility we have to respect and obey all legitimate authority. The *Catechism* provides very specific examples: it is obligatory, for example, "to pay taxes, to exercise the right to vote, and to defend one's country" (#2240). Sometimes, however, we must refuse obedience to civil authorities when its dictates violate our consciences.

Recommended Reading

Articles 2168–257.

Commentary 32: The Fifth Commandment

Q. Are there many applications of the fifth commandment to everyday life?

A. Yes, very many. "You shall not kill," of course, prohibits the direct and intentional murder of another human being. However, the *Catechism* in its treatment of that commandment also covers such topics as legitimate self-defense; abortion; euthanasia; the use of drugs; scientific, medical, or psychological experiments; organ transplants; terrorism; sterilization; autopsies; suicide; cremation; free gift of bodily organs; war; conscientious objection; and the contemporary use, sale, or storage of arms.

Q. Is there a basic principle governing all those diverse situations?

A. The fundamental truth involved with these concerns states quite simply, yet starkly, "Human life is sacred." A relatively recent Church document quoted in the *Catechism* cites the reason for this sacredness. Human life, the text maintains, from its beginning involves the creative action of God. Moreover, that life remains forever in a special relationship with the Creator, who is its sole end. God alone, the *Catechism* goes on to say, is the Lord of life from its beginning until its end. No one can under any circumstance claim for herself or himself the right directly to destroy an innocent human being.

Q. What about the death penalty?

A. Self-defense, for individuals and for public authority, is legitimate and sometimes a duty. Such self-preservation, personally and for society, may justify the indirect wounding or even killing of the aggressor. The *Catechism* acknowledges "the right and duty of legitimate public authority to punish malefactors by means of penalties commensurate with the gravity of the crime, not excluding, in cases of extreme gravity, the death penalty" (#2266).

The U.S. Conference of Bishops and local bishops, while recognizing that right and duty, have nevertheless opposed the death penalty in this nation because of what they judge to be its unjust application.

Pope John Paul II in his encyclical *The Gospel of Life* has further restricted the uses of the death penalty, arguing that cases when it would be justified are "very rare if not practically nonexistent."

Q. What about abortion?

A. Not surprisingly, the *Catechism* teaches that abortion willed either as an end or means is gravely contrary to the moral law. From the first moment of existence (at conception), a human being must be recognized as having the rights of a person, above all the right to life.

Moreover, the text maintains that this teaching "Since the first century...has not changed and remains unchangeable" (#2271).

Sometimes pro-choice Catholics argue that the thrust of the Second Vatican Council allows greater freedom of conscience in this matter. In developing their points, they apparently select some passages and ignore others. The *Catechism* corrects that inaccurate approach by quoting the words of the Vatican II bishops: "Life must be protected with the utmost care from the moment of conception: abortion and infanticide are abominable crimes" (#2271).

Q. What about euthanasia?

A. Direct euthanasia, putting an end to the lives of handicapped, sick, or dying persons, is termed morally unacceptable. We must give ordinary care to sick persons. However, discontinuing medical procedures that are burdensome, dangerous, extraordinary, or disproportionate to the expected outcome can be legitimate. The *Catechism,* however, does not resolve the current controverted question about the moral obligation of tubular nutrition and hydration for those unable to eat or drink. We may do this, but must we? An unanswered issue.

The listing of topics covered and these three samples should indicate just how current and practical is this particular section of the Catechism.

Recommended Reading

Articles 2258–330.

Commentary 33: The Sixth and Ninth Commandments

Q. Do the commandments deal only with actions?

A. Most of the precepts in the Decalogue seem solely to address deeds we do or fail to do. However, all of them have an implicit inner dimension and some even an explicit interior aspect. For example, the sixth and seventh commandments center on actions, and the ninth and tenth concentrate on attitudes related to those actions.

Q. Are there essential principles behind the Church's teaching on sexuality?

A. Yes. The first sketches an ideal: "Sexuality...becomes personal and truly human when it is integrated into the relationship of one person to another, in the complete and lifelong mutual gift of a man and woman" (#2337). The second states a practical application: "The deliberate use of the sexual faculty, for whatever reason, outside of marriage is essentially contrary to its purpose" (#2352). Those principles have enormous ramifications.

Q. What, then, are some applications of "You shall not commit adultery"?

A. In addition to adultery, which refers to marital infidelity, the sixth and ninth commandments encompass, among other actions, masturbation, fornication, pornography, prostitution, incest, homosexuality, cohabitation, artificial conception and contraception, modesty, and divorce.

Q. Isn't this too demanding for today's world?

A. Perhaps, but the Church teaches that all the baptized are called to live a chaste life, whether married or not. That means a lifelong and exacting effort at self-mastery. However, here are the alternatives: "Either [we] govern [our] passions and find peace or [we] let [ourselves] be dominated by them and become unhappy" (#2339).

Q. How does this apply to engaged or cohabitating couples?

A. They are called to reserve for marriage the expressions of affection that belong to married love. "The sexual act must take place exclusively within marriage. Outside of marriage it always constitutes a grave sin and excludes one from sacramental communion" (#2390).

Many engaged or cohabitating couples will disagree with or at least find this teaching difficult to accept. In a large Midwest archdiocese, to illustrate, a survey of five hundred couples who had completed its marriage preparation programs revealed that 40 percent were living together and 90 percent were sexually active with each other.

Q. Does this principle prohibit masturbation?

A. The *Catechism* maintains that masturbation is an "intrinsically and gravely disordered action" (#2352). However, it then goes on to stress that a person's moral culpability for such an action may be lessened or even eliminated because of personal, social, or psychological factors.

Certain Catholic moral theologians in the United States have attacked that position, arguing that objectively it is not wrong or at least not seriously wrong.

This type of theological dispute occurs on many applications in these moral matters. The Church strives to be consistent, upholding an objective ideal, yet showing a compassion for those who do not live up to this norm. Some theologians simply reject such objective moral commands.

Q. Would that discrepancy hold true in the area of homosexuality?

A. Yes. The Church states that "homosexual acts are intrinsically disordered." But it also subsequently stresses that men and women with deep-seated homosexual tendencies "must be accepted with respect, compassion, and sensitivity. Every sign of unjust discrimination in their regard should be avoided" (#2357–58).

In general, homosexual individuals find this teaching offensive, despite the *Catechism's* compassionate tone.

Q. Does the Church consider sex as bad or ugly?

A. No. On the contrary, it maintains that sexual acts in marriage are noble and honorable, foster self-giving, and enrich spouses with joy and gratitude.

Recommended Reading

Articles 2331–400, 2514–33.

Commentary 34: The Seventh Commandment

Q. Does the seventh commandment really apply to the average person?

A. Absolutely. "You should not steal" may seem quite limited in its scope, but that command has widespread applications. The mandate goes far beyond petty thefts committed during one's youth or armed robberies carried out by drug addicts. Anyone who reads the seventeen pages or sixty-two articles (2401–63) from the *Catechism* about this commandment will very likely feel uneasy, annoyed, or both.

Q. What are some of those practical applications?

A. The *Catechism* cites these examples of unjustly taking and keeping the property of others: deliberately retaining goods lent or found; business fraud; work poorly done; tax evasion; forgery of checks and invoices; excessive expenses and waste; paying unjust wages; and forcing up prices by taking advantage of another's ignorance or hardship.

Q. Is there a basic principle behind the *Catechism*'s teaching about stealing?

A. Yes. The text begins by stating the fundamental notion of stewardship. God, according to Genesis 1:26–29, entrusted the earth and its resources to humankind with the command to take care of them, master them by labor, and enjoy their fruits.

It upholds the right and necessity of private property for the welfare and security of individuals. However, it cautions that this right is not absolute and must be balanced against the needs of society or the common good.

Those two notions and the tension that often exists between them occur repeatedly in the *Catechism*'s discussion of the seventh commandment.

Q. Are gifted persons obligated to share what they possess?

A. Yes. An older adage, *"Noblesse oblige,"* captures the *Catechism*'s teaching. Those who possess goods of production like land, buildings, or personal skills should employ them to bring about the greatest benefit for the largest number. Those who possess goods for use and consumption should employ them with moderation, always reserving part for guests, the sick, and the poor.

Q. How does the *Catechism* deal with gambling?

A. Games of chance or wagers (for example, bingo or betting) are not, the text states, in themselves contrary to justice. But they become morally unacceptable when persons gamble with resources necessary for their own or others' needs. Moreover, the passion for gambling can become an addiction that enslaves us, a situation contrary to God's plan and thus immoral.

Q. Will animal-rights advocates reject the *Catechism*'s guidance?

A. Quite likely. Animals, like plants and inanimate beings, are, the text maintains, for the good of humanity past, present, and future. We must treat them with kindness. However, since they have been designed for human beings, they can be used for food and clothing as well as for medical and scientific experimentation, provided this is done within reasonable limits. Furthermore, it warns about spending money on animals that should go for the relief of human misery, and about giving animals the love or affection due only to human beings.

Q. Do we have a special obligation for the poor?

A. The official Church calls us to have a preferential love for the poor, an attitude incompatible with an immoderate love or selfish use of riches.

Recommended Reading

Articles 2401–63.

Commentary 35: The Eighth and Tenth Commandments

Q. What is the meaning of the eighth commandment?

A. "You shall not bear false witness against your neighbor" deals positively with truth and negatively with falsehood. God has given us the ability to communicate. To employ that talent for conveying the truth is to use this gift well. To tell a lie or deliberately deceive another is, therefore, an objectively evil action.

Q. Does this commandment have significant current ramifications?

A. Yes. For example, contemporary trial debates, deliberate government or business misinformation, and media misrepresentations often seem to color or put a desired spin on events rather than to bring forth the truth in all its clarity.

Q. How hard is it to always speak the truth?

A. Very. The letter of James contains in chapter three a section on the "power of the tongue." The author states, "If anyone does not fall short in speech, that individual is a perfect person, able to bridle the whole body also."

This assertion obviously implies that it is difficult, impossible actually without grace, always to be truthful. If George Washington never did tell a lie, he must have been, according to this definition, a remarkably perfect person.

Q. Do those in court have unique obligations to be truthful?

A. Making a statement contrary to the truth constitutes false witness and, under oath, becomes perjury. Such violations of the eighth commandment can cause enormous harm to others. They contribute to the condemning of innocent persons, to the exonerating of guilty people, and to the increasing of punishment for those accused or found guilty. Thus these offenses severely violate justice.

Q. Is neighborhood gossip or rumor spreading forbidden by this commandment?

A. It prohibits any attitude or word that mars the reputation of others. The more common ways in which this can be done are

- Rash judgment—When we even tacitly assume as true, without sufficient foundation, a neighbor's moral fault.
- Detraction—When we disclose, without an objectively valid reason, another's failings and faults to persons unaware of those shortcomings.
- Calumny—When we, with untrue remarks, harm the reputation of others or lead people to make false judgments about others.

Centuries ago, St. Ignatius of Loyola gave this practical advice: "Every good Christian ought to be more ready to give a favorable interpretation to another's statement than to condemn it."

The *Catechism* echoes that sentiment by urging everyone to interpret insofar as possible the thoughts, words, and deeds of others in a favorable way.

Q. Must we tell everyone everything?

A. No. The right to information or the communication of the truth is not absolute. Therefore, we must judge in particular situations whether or not it is appropriate to reveal the truth to someone who asks for this information. "The good and safety of others, respect for privacy, and the common good are sufficient reasons for being silent about what ought not to be known or for making use of a discreet language....No one is bound to reveal the truth to someone who does not have the right to know it" (#2489).

Q. Could you summarize the tenth commandment?

A. "You shall not covet anything that belongs to your neighbor" in essence concerns the human heart and the greed or envy that can enslave us.

Recommended Reading

Articles 2464–513, 2534–57.

PART FOUR: CHRISTIAN PRAYER
Section One: Prayer in the Christian Life

Commentary 36: Prayer

Q. Is the end in sight?

A. Yes. We have just completed that lengthy part three, "Life in Christ," which encompassed 190 pages and covered articles 1691–2557. Our final task, which will take four weeks, addresses a shorter but inspirational part four, "Christian Prayer." Articles 2558–865 treat this subject and will bring our nearly year long discussion to an end.

Q. What is prayer?

A. The *Catechism* cites a saint for an answer to this question, and a relatively modern one at that. St. Thérèse of Lisieux described prayer in this way: "For me, prayer is a surge of the heart; it is a simple look turned toward heaven, it is a cry of recognition and love, embracing both trial and joy."

Q. How does the *Catechism* examine the subject of prayer?

A. The *Catechism* divides its discussion into two sections: The first, "Prayer in the Christian Life," outlines the ancient biblical tradition of prayer and then offers some practical suggestions on how to pray. The authors of this portion clearly are well informed about current insights into a life of prayer. The second, "The Lord's Prayer: 'Our Father,'" is a rich meditation on the prayer Christ gave us.

Q. Does prayer come from the mind, the Spirit, the soul, or the heart?

A. Prayer really starts from God. It is our response to God's love and blessings. We express faith, gratitude, and dependence upon the Lord for the gifts given and needed.

Keeping that clarification in mind, we can then state that it is the whole person who prays. However, we do refer to prayer as originating in our mind, soul, Spirit, or heart.

The location mentioned most often in the Bible (more than a thousand times) is the heart. The heart is the place to which I withdraw, my hidden center, a space beyond the grasp of our own reason and of others, the place of decision, an area deeper than our psychic drives, the place of truth, encounter, and covenant. Only God's Spirit can penetrate the human heart and know it fully.

Q. Are there many biblical examples of prayer in the *Catechism?*

A. Yes. It first looks at the Old Testament and briefly notes the connection of prayer with creation, Abraham, Jacob, Moses, David, and Elijah, as well as other prophets. The *Catechism* devotes particular attention to the psalms. These many prayer songs were eventually collected into the five books of what we call the Psalter or "Praises." While useful for personal or individual prayer, the 150 psalms have more significantly become the core of the Church's Liturgy of the Hours.

Q. How do you pray the Psalter when the tone of a particular psalm does not match your mood?

A. That conflict is easily resolved when praying personally or individually. Most prayer books with psalms have classified them according to general themes— petition, praise, forgiveness, and so on. One simply selects the psalm that best corresponds to the current inner attitude or feeling.

That conflict is not so easily resolved when praying the Liturgy of the Hours with assigned psalms that do not reflect our present mood. Nevertheless, if we remember that this is the official prayer of the entire Church throughout the world, then we can raise our sights and recognize that someone on this planet is at the very moment joyful or burdened, even if we are neither. We thus pray in their name.

Q. What about the New Testament and prayer?

A. The *Catechism* presents sections from the New Testament entitled "Jesus prays," "Jesus teaches us how to pray," "Jesus hears our prayer," and "The prayer of the Virgin Mary."

Recommended Reading

Articles 2558–622.

Commentary 37: Types and Places of Prayer

Q. What does the word "blessing" mean in Christian prayer?

A. The term *bless* has a double connotation. We speak of God's blessing us or bestowing upon us a variety of gifts that fulfill our needs and wants. However, we also "bless" or praise God for those many graces and blessings.

The notion of God's blessing us is familiar enough. However, for most people the concept of our "blessing" God seems novel and awkward.

The prayers at the preparation of the gifts during Mass illustrate this blessing notion of prayer.

Q. Is the *ACTS* notion of prayer still appropriate?

A. In religious instruction classes, teachers have often used the acronym *ACTS* to explain the multiple dimensions of appropriate prayer. According to this formula, good prayer includes adoration, contrition, thanksgiving, and supplication.

The *Catechism* does not employ that particular formula, but it explains the various ingredients of sound prayer: adoration, petition, intercession, thanksgiving, praise, and requests for forgiveness.

Q. How do petition and intercession differ?

A. In petition we "ask, beseech, plead, invoke, entreat, cry out, even 'struggle in prayer'" (#2629). Intercession is, more specifically, a prayer of petition on behalf of others. It mirrors the Master, since Jesus, as the book of Hebrews relates, "always lives to make intercession for us."

Q. May we get individual and local in our petitions and intercessions?

A. Yes. God knows our needs and wishes. Consequently, we mention people, places, and situations in our prayers not to inform God, but to stir up our own faith and fervor. Prayer is usually more intense when we pray for a particular intention.

The *Catechism* states, "*Every need* can become the object of petition" (#2633). Moreover, it declares that any event may be an offering of thanksgiving. Finally, the *Catechism* reminds us that our intercessions as Christians "recognize no boundaries" (#2636).

Q. Will we find practical suggestions for prayer in the *Catechism*?

A. Many. For example, in touching upon prayer to Jesus, the *Catechism* mentions several titles of the Lord we might use: "Son of God, Word of God, Lord, Savior, Lamb of God, King, Beloved Son, Son of the Virgin, Good Shepherd, our Life, our Light, our Hope, our Resurrection, Friend of Humankind." Nevertheless, it notes that one name or title contains everything: "Jesus." Furthermore, the *Catechism* declares that "the invocation of the holy name of Jesus is the simplest way of praying always" (#2668).

Q. What is the "Jesus Prayer"?

A. For repetitious prayer, many people have for centuries used the following formula, biblically based and from an Eastern tradition: "Lord, Jesus Christ, Son of God, have mercy on us sinners."

Q. Does the *Catechism* encourage prayer to the Holy Spirit?

A. To quote: "The Church invites us to call upon the Holy Spirit every day, especially at the beginning and the end of every important action" (#2670). The new Bishop James Moynihan of Syracuse has included a symbol of the Holy Spirit on his coat of arms. He also recalls boyhood moments of praying to the Holy Spirit at his mother's insistence every day after Communion. That early initiation formed a habit within him that continues today.

Q. Where is the best place to pray?

A. We can pray anywhere. The *Catechism* does mention the suitability of a church, especially as the privileged place for adoration of Christ's presence in the Blessed Sacrament. It also cites other locations like "prayer corners" at home, monasteries, and shrines. Spiritual directors, recommended by the *Catechism,* are helpful in discerning for us the best place and way to pray.

Recommended Reading

Articles 2623–96.

Commentary 38: The Life of Prayer

Q. How often must we pray?

A. The Bible tells us to pray always, to pray constantly, and to pray without ceasing. An ancient teacher in the Church put it this way: "'We must remember God mor often than we draw breath'" (#2697).

Q. Isn't that physically, or at least practically, impossible?

A. It depends upon one's definition of prayer. If we speak of prayer as composure of the heart or walking in the presence of God, then those admonitions are more doable.

The Church, however, seeking to nurture this continual prayer, proposes certain rhythms for our inner life. Morning and evening prayer, grace at meals, and the Liturgy of the Hours are examples of that. Sunday prayer, especially centered around the Eucharist, is another illustration. Celebration of feasts like Christmas, Easter, and Pentecost are a third way in which we can grow in the practice of praying constantly.

Q. Are reading or reciting prayers valuable?

A. In such vocal prayer we use either silently or aloud the words of others to help us pray. The phrases may be biblical (like the psalms) or official Church prayers (like those for the sick) or individually developed texts (like approved litanies).

Because we are bodily beings, these outward prayers give expression to our inner, or spiritual, sentiments. They also deepen them. But in the words of St. John Chrysostom, "'Whether or not our prayer is heard depends not on the number of words, but on the fervor of our souls'" (#2700).

Q. What is meditation or contemplative prayer?

A. They are similar but distinct forms of prayer.

In meditation, we use thought, imagination, emotion, and desire, sometimes with the help of books or other visual aids, to imagine a Christian scene or truth and confront ourselves with it.

Contemplation, on the other hand, is more of a "close sharing between friends" and "means taking time frequently to be alone with him who we know loves us" (#2709). This usually entails less use of those energetic tools above and is, instead, a reflective gaze of faith, which fixes upon Jesus.

The humble Curé of Ars summarized his contemplative prayer in these words, "'I look at him and he looks at me'" (#2715).

Q. Do people ever experience dryness or darkness in prayer?

A. Those who pray regularly encounter from time to time occasional and sometimes prolonged dark or dry periods. These are normally temptations, purifications, or tests and not warning signals that something is amiss in our spiritual lives. Prayer is a battle and a quest. Darkness and dryness are part of that struggle.

Q. Are prayers answered?

A. Always, but not necessarily in the way we expect or hope. A spiritual writer from the past commented, "'Do not be troubled if you do not immediately receive from God what you ask; for God desires to do something even greater for you, while you cling to him in prayer'" (#2737).

Q. When is the best time to pray?

A. Someone wrote, "'It is possible to offer fervent prayer even while walking in public or strolling alone, or seated in your shop,...while buying or selling,...or even while cooking'" (#2743). Those words sound as if they came from a contemporary commentator. St. John Chrysostom penned them in the fourth century.

Recommended Reading
Articles 2697–758.

Section Two: The Lord's Prayer: "Our Father"

Commentary 39: "Our Father"

Q. Where did the "Our Father" come from?

A. We call this the Lord's Prayer because Jesus the Lord gave it to us through his first followers. Those early disciples asked Christ to teach them how to pray. In response, the Master taught them the "Our Father." In St. Luke's account, the prayer contains a brief text of five petitions. St. Matthew's Gospel provides a more developed version of seven petitions. Catholic liturgical services use the formula from St. Matthew's account.

Q. Is there a Catholic and Protestant "Our Father"?

A. That may seem to be the case. Catholics generally conclude the Lord's Prayer with "...deliver us from evil, Amen." Protestants customarily end the "Our Father" with "For thine is the Kingdom, the power, and the glory...." In an ecumenical setting, that may create an awkward situation. Catholics stop, and Protestants keep going.

Q. Why is there this difference?

A. The shorter Catholic version is strictly biblical. In the early Christian centuries, however, liturgies often added a doxology, or phrase of praise and adoration, at the conclusion of the "Our Father." Ancient documents like the *Didache* and *Apostolic Constitutions* mention that addition. The longer Protestant version contains this developed doxology. Today, in a nonliturgical prayer service involving both Catholics and Protestants, we would tend to use the expanded "Our Father."

Q. Don't we recite or sing a similar doxology in the Mass?

A. Yes. The Roman Missal revised after the Second Vatican Council developed the last petition of the "Our Father" with a prayer technically titled the embolism: "Deliver us, Lord, from every evil and grant us peace...." The doxology we have discussed concludes that expanded petition. Those who constructed the revised Mass clearly understood the complexity of this matter and created a compromise that incorporates both features—the purely scriptural "Our Father" with the ancient and revered but nonbiblical doxology.

Q. Does the Church hold the Lord's Prayer in special esteem?

A. These quotes from early Catholic Christian writers underscore how important the "Our Father" is in the Church's tradition. The Lord's Prayer "'is truly the summary of the whole gospel'" (#2761). "'Run through all the words of the holy prayers [in Scripture], and I do not think that you will find anything in them that is not contained and included in the Lord's Prayer'" (#2762). "'The Lord's Prayer is the most perfect of prayers...'" (#2763).

Q. Are there current examples of the "Our Father" in the Church's worship?

A. In both baptism and confirmation, especially of adults, the handing over of the "Our Father" to new Catholics is a significant gesture. They now can speak to God with God's word. In the Mass, the "Our Father" is a bridge between our pure worship of God through the eucharistic prayer and our preparation for the gift of Christ's coming in Communion. Finally, whenever we bring the Eucharist to the ill or homebound, we always recite the Lord's Prayer because of its link with the Bread of Life.

Q. What is the significance of the "our"?

A. We can see a twofold meaning in the "our" connected with "Father." First, we address a God who is both the Father of Jesus and our Father. Second, we address the Father not so much as individuals but as members of a community. Christ's dying and rising bind us to one another as brothers and sisters in the Lord and enable us all to call God, "Father."

Q. Will some feminists be offended by the emphasis on the prayer and title of God as "our Father"?

A. Probably. The *Catechism,* however, reminds us that the notion of God as Father transcends all human categories. In visualizing or addressing God we must, therefore, purify and rise above the paternal or maternal images that we have absorbed from our personal or cultural history.

Q. What does "who art in heaven" mean?

A. This biblical phrase does *not* mean a place or space, but a way of being. It does *not* mean that God is distant, but rather that God is majestic. Our Father is *not* elsewhere but transcends everything we can imagine. God is in fact close to the humble of heart and dwells within those who are holy.

Recommended Reading

Articles 2759–802.

Commentary 40: Seven Petitions, Citations, and Subject Index

Q. Do the petitions of the Lord's Prayer have a double movement?

A. Yes. After placing ourselves in the divine presence and adoring the Lord, we direct seven petitions to God our Father. Three move immediately to the Creator: thy name, thy kingdom, thy will. The four others pertain directly to people on earth: "Give us...forgive us...lead us not...deliver us."

Q. How do we "hallow" God's name?

A. *Hallow* literally means "to make holy." Only God causes or makes us holy. Therefore, in one sense with this statement we praise God for the divine holiness. In another sense, we are asking God to make us holy. Thus, God's glory will be made evident through the holiness of men and women who follow Christ.

Q. When will the kingdom come?

A. The kingdom of God lies ahead of us. The phrase "Thy kingdom come" refers primarily to the final coming of God's reign through Christ's return at the end of the world. However, God calls us to prepare now for that moment by working for peace with justice here on earth.

Q. Is God's will for us clear?

A. God's will for us can be simply stated, but complex and challenging to carry out. Jesus came that all might be saved through believing in him and loving one another as he has loved us.

Q. Does the *Catechism* encourage daily Mass?

A. Yes, at different occasions and for various reasons. The bread we ask for covers all our material and spiritual needs and includes, particularly, the Bread of Life, or the Eucharist. We seek and hope for just enough to take us through today.

St. Augustine said, "'The Eucharist is our daily bread....the readings you hear each day in church and the hymns you hear and sing. All these are necessities for our pilgrimage'" (#2837).

Q. Why is there such stress on forgiving?

A. The *Catechism* employs unusual words for an official text. It describes the teaching about God's mercy and our need to forgive as "astonishing" and "daunting" truths (#2838–40). Unless we are willing to forgive, then we will not experience God's profound peace within us. We do not have the power to forget an offense, but God does supply us the ability to forgive an injury.

Q. How does the *Catechism* conclude?

A. The text finishes as does the Lord's Prayer with "Amen," which means "So be it," "Yes," "I agree," "I accept what has been taught and said."

Q. Are there significant references at the end of the *Catechism*?

A. The citations are extensive: for example, Scripture references (thirty-two pages), ecumenical councils (seven pages), papal teachings (five pages), Church writers (eleven pages). In addition, there is a forty-seven–page subject index, which makes it relatively easy to locate topics by article numbers.

Q. Is our study finished?

A. Yes. Congratulations on completing this forty-session commentary on the *Catechism!*

Recommended Reading

Articles 2803–65; 114 pages of reference citations.

SECTION 3
QUESTIONS FOR GROUP DISCUSSION

THESE QUESTIONS CAN be used for group discussions after the participants have read the recommended sections of the *Catechism*.

A Brief Overview

- Will the use of exclusive language damage the impact of the *Catechism* on the Church in the United States?
- Is there confusion about current Catholic teaching concerning our beliefs and behavioral norms?
- Can you think of examples showing how the Church follows a middle course in its beliefs and moral teachings?
- Are there divergent attitudes about theology and spirituality in parishes? Do we have different views about who God is, what the Church should be, and how we pray?
- Will many Catholics oppose the Church's teachings on premarital sex and acted-out homosexuality? Will many Americans?

Part One: The Profession of Faith

- Is there a renewed interest in Mary and Marian devotion today? Do you have any personal examples of this?
- In what way would you see a feminine influence operating in the Church today?
- Do you see God as a powerful force or a caring person?
- Can you give some illustrations of the divine and human element of the Church in the United States today?
- Briefly describe the person you see/imagine when you think of God.
- Describe your image of what Jesus is like. Which qualities of his do you relate to the best or appreciate the most and why?
- If you had the opportunity to share your beliefs about Jesus Christ with a person who was actively seeking God and truth, what would you say?

Part Two: Celebration of the Christian Mystery

- Do you think most Catholics believe or are conscious that Christ is present and at work in the sacraments?
- Should confirmation occur when it does now (about two years into high school) or before first Communion as it was in the early Church?
- Have you had any experiences of healing through reconciliation, anointing of the sick, or the laying on of hands in prayer?

- Are you comfortable blessing your children, or would you be comfortable reading a blessing over them?
- Think for a moment about your experiences of the seven sacraments. Choose one sacrament and comment on an experience you had that constituted a deepening of your faith in Christ. How did this event bring fresh insight and life to you?

Part Three: Life in Christ

- Are there objectively wrong actions, or does morality depend solely upon the individual person's intention and circumstances?
- Is the Church cruel or compassionate in its teaching on homosexuality?
- Do most Catholics consider missing Mass on Sunday something serious?
- What do you think about physician-assisted suicide?
- How would you vote on a referendum about the death penalty?
- What do you think is the most pressing moral issue today that the Church must address and why?
- If you were to design a public-relations effort regarding Catholic Christian morality for a parish or school or the Church at large, what would the slogan be and how would you put the ideas across?
- What reasons do you think the current American social climate provides for a need to return to and reemphasize Biblical moral values?

Part Four: Christian Prayer

- How would you define prayer for yourself?
- Do you have a special place, time, or way of praying?
- What is your reaction when your prayers are not answered?
- Have you experienced dark or dry times of prayer?
- Which do you prefer, praying alone or with others? Why?
- Examine the Lord's Prayer for a moment. What word or words express to you a truth that you feel deeply in your life right now?
- What is one of your favorite prayers and why?

ABOUT THE AUTHOR

FATHER JOSEPH CHAMPLIN recently celebrated his fortieth anniversary as a parish priest for the diocese of Syracuse in New York, where he currently serves as the rector of its Cathedral.

In addition to his pastoral work, he has traveled nearly two million miles here and abroad, lecturing on various Church topics. Moreover, Father Champlin has written more than forty books, with twenty million copies of his publications in print. These include the well-known and long-time bestseller *Together for Life* (also available in Spanish from Liguori Publications) and recent titles *A Thoughtful Word, A Healing Touch: A Guide for Visiting the Sick; With Hearts Light As Feathers: The Sacrament of Reconciliation for Children; The Visionary Leader; What It Means to Be Catholic; Meeting the Merciful Christ; The Marginal Catholic;* and *The Stations of the Cross with Pope John Paul II* (Liguori).

He has also produced several audio-visual items, including a new video *The Heart of Stewardship: Sacrificial Giving* and an audio-cassette album *A Pastor Looks at the New Catechism.*

More Catechism companions from Liguori...
The essential reference to the faith

CATECHISM OF THE CATHOLIC CHURCH
Libreria Editrice Vaticana
co–published by Liguori Publications

Unlike other versions of the *Catechism*, Liguori's includes the Index of Citations. This index cross–references the *Catechism* with sacred Scripture and important Church documents. Now available at a reduced price! **$9.95, paperback • $19.95, hardcover**

*Also available in Spanish...***$9.95** (paperback only)

HOW TO READ THE CATECHISM OF THE
CATHOLIC CHURCH FOLLOWING THE LITURGICAL YEAR
by Bernabe Dalmau

This easy-to-understand guide recommends short but suitable excerpts which will allow use of the *Catechism* devotionally, and provides a practical introduction for anyone who wants to "go slow." In addition, there is a step-by-step plan for each day of the liturgical year. **$2.95**

BEACONS OF LIGHT
Profiles of Ecclesiastical Writers Cited in the Catechism
by Louis Miller, C.SS.R.

Short biographical sketches and excerpts from the writings of 73 "ecclesiastical writers" cited in the *Catechism*. A guide to the accomplishments of this diverse group. **$4.95**

WHAT YOU SHOULD KNOW ABOUT
THE CATECHISM OF THE CATHOLIC CHURCH
by Charlene Altemose, MSC

An indispensable starting point for basic understanding, intelligent reading, and practical use of the *Catechism*. It carefully explains the *Catechism* without getting bogged down in theology or academics. **$1.95**

Order from your local bookstore or write
Liguori Publications
Box 060, Liguori, MO 63057-9999
(Please add $2 for postage and handling for orders $9.99 and under;
$3 for orders between $10 and $14.99; $4 for orders $15 and over.)